20 December 1898

With love to Dad,

A graphic story of life as
a child between the front lines,
a reminder of what it may have
been like for distant relatives in Alsace.

Happy Birthday!

Tomiko

TOMI
A CHILDHOOD UNDER THE NAZIS

Aged three, in the Orangerie in Strasbourg, 1935.

TOMI

A CHILDHOOD UNDER THE NAZIS

TOMI UNGERER

A division of

THE ROBERTS RINEHART PUBLISHING GROUP

Boulder • Dublin • London • Sydney

Published in the United States and Canada by TomiCo
The Roberts Rinehart Publishing Group
6309 Monarch Park Place
Niwot, Colorado 80503
TEL 303.652.2685
FAX 303.652.2689
www.robertsrinehart.com

Distributed to the trade by Publishers Group West

Published in Ireland by TomiCo
Town House and Country House Publishers
Trinity House, Charleston Road
Ranelagh, Dublin 6

Published in the UK by TomiCo
Airlift Book Company
8 the Arena, Mollison Avenue, Enfield
Middlesex EN3 7NJ England

Published in Australia and New Zealand by TomiCo
Peribo PTY Ltd.
58 Beaumont Road
Mount Kuring - GAI
NSW 2080 Australia

International Standard Book Number 1-57098-163-9
Library of Congress Catalog Card Number: 98-86189

Printed in Hong Kong

10 9 8 7 6 5 4 3 2 1

Ich bin und heiße Hans Ungerer.
Ich werde der Wanderer sein.

Schulheft, 1. Halbjahr 1943

I am and am called Hans Ungerer
I shall be the wanderer

(OUT OF A SCHOOLBOOK, 1943)

LOSS JEDER WE'N ER ESCH
SO BLEISCH DU WIE DU BESCH

Let everyone be what they are
And you will be what you are

(JEWISH-ALSATIAN SAYING)

This book is dedicated to my friend André Bord,
Ministre des Anciens Combattants, head of the Franco-German
Commission, member of the French Resistance, twice arrested by
the Gestapo, twice escaped—he is still among us to show us that
you can turn resentment into harmony,

and to Jack Van Zandt and Jeanne Schuster who with
dedication made this English edition possible.

ACKNOWLEDGMENTS

My thanks go to Thérèse Willer, curator of the Centre Tomi Ungerer in Strasbourg, Christianne Sigel, Sylviane Poirier and Bernard Reumaux for the French edition, Paul Wilsdorf, Patrick Hamm, Jean Vermeil, René Ohl, Francis Catella, Marcel Pini, Christian Rebert, and my German editor Winfried Steffan.

My thanks also to Celia Lowenstein, who produced the film "Fascination Fascism," and to Francis Rosenstiel and Freddy Raphael for their participation.

This book was first written in French and published as *À la Guerre Comme à la Guerre* in 1991, and was an edited version of what is now the English-language edition. I then reconceived it in German as *Die Gedanken Sind Frei*, which translates as Thoughts are Free, the title of my favorite German folksong (not sung under the Nazis). It was meant to be read by both adults and children, and I was given the nicest compliment by a mother who told me that her six-year-old boy slept with it under his pillow. The French and German editions were illustrated with documents I had collected during the war, along with my writings and drawings from childhood that my mother had saved.

After the book appeared, I was showered with boxes full of documents and books concerning this period. Many people, especially secondhand bookdealers, entrusted me with heretofore hidden or forgotten testimonies of a painful, ignoble past. This edition, rewritten in English, has been enlarged with many documents selected from these donations.

The documentation used in my book is quite unique, depicting in detail the finicky aspect of a huge propaganda machine. On the other hand, the pictures that I drew at a crucial age, at the price of my innocence, constitute an opposing view, equally distorted.

History is a matter of facts. Many historians are out to prove something. My book doesn't prove anything; it only tells what I witnessed as a child with no prejudice. Historians can argue about opinions, but no one can deny what I saw with my own eyes.

In New York, I had a Jewish friend. He had been born in Auschwitz, where his parents had died, and where he had survived the first years of his life. What are my anecdotes compared to such terrible tragedy?

My family and I were spared the worst effects of the war. Thanks to my mother's cleverness and good sense we lived a fairly normal everyday life in spite of the Nazi regime. Therefore this book, on the surface, might appear to be a trivialization of the great dramas of misery, torture, and violence. But if I speak of this period in the way one would speak of a summer vacation, it is because as a young boy it seemed, with the detachment of childhood, as if I was watching a spectacle, in the same way, perhaps, that my children watch television today.

Living through those times, however, has had a profound effect on me in my adult life and I have become, in my own way, a passionate advocate of peace and nonviolence. My art, books, posters, and pamphlets exist to testify how, in an obsessive way, I have been inspired by the horrors of injustice and violence. And I have learned that there is ultimately no antidote to prejudice, to hatred, to injustice, if it is not to be found in the voice of each person's conscience, which tells us what we must do.

*I drew this map of France for my geography lesson during the occupation—
Alsace is missing. After the war I drew a map of Germany, and there Alsace
is also missing. This is the ultimate proof that Alsace doesn't exist!*

Alsace is wedged between France and Germany, a buffer zone along the Rhine. Its fate and history is unlike that of any other group of people in Europe. Alsatians have a strong identity, yet there is no such thing as an Alsatian race. Our melting pot has, over time, integrated Celts, Romans, Franks, *"alemanni"* (who brought us the language we speak), Helvetii, French, German, Italians, and Jews.

After the Thirty Years War (1618–1648) during which Alsace lost one-third of its population (massacred by the Swedish troops of Gustav II Adolf), we became French for the first time. Before that, Alsace had been a province within the Holy Roman Empire, a confederation of free cities with virtually no ruling aristocracy. In 1262 Strasbourg had established the first democratic constitution in Europe, overthrowing the power of the bishops.

During the Renaissance Alsace became one of the greatest centers of cultural effervescence, a center of humanism. Printing was invented here. And as a society with mercantile traditions, and no princes to support either the Protestant or Catholic causes, it hardly suffered from the religious wars that plagued the rest of Europe. Even today some churches are shared by both religions.

This strip of land between the Vosges mountains and the Rhine, coveted for its wealth and prosperity as well as for its strategic position, was at various times throughout history controlled by either the Germans or the French. My grandmother changed nationalities in 1871, 1918, 1940, and 1945. The French and Germans left their imprints by showering the Alsatians with monuments, palaces, and numerous institutions. For instance, after 1871 the Cathedral of St. Paul was erected in Strasbourg by Kaiser Wilhelm. There, every Sunday, his Protestant garrison would be marched for spiritual training.

Having to adapt ourselves to constant changes has given the Alsatians a great sense of insecurity. To whom do we belong? We turned into chameleons, changing colors—or languages—to survive. I have a friend born after World War II who only learned to speak French, as Alsatian and German were frowned upon, if not forbidden, in school. This friend's mother had a stroke a few years ago; her loving son was at her bedside when she regained consciousness, but her French was gone, and to this day she can only express herself in German.

After years of occupation, Alsace no longer has to survive under the German boot or the French slipper. We are simply part of Europe. Alsatians are born Europeans and it is only right that Strasbourg (not to be confused with Salzburg) is the seat of the European Council and Parliament, and the Court of Human Rights.

Alsace never won or lost a war—our neighbors did, using us as cannon fodder. Alsatians loathe violence, for whoever suffers inflicted wars seeks peace. Peace is good for business, and as the "Germans" of France (which is better than being the "French" of Germany), Alsatians have, after Parisians, the highest per capita income—and the most Michelin stars—of any French region.

Our sense of balance can only be fulfilled when both sides of the scale are empty. Berlin had one wall. We had three: a French one, a German one, and, still, our own wailing wall. And although there has been a lot of bloody water under our bridges, they, like the Alsatian people, are still very much there.

My illustration for a German folksong. The caption reads: "I shall try my luck marching."

In the Orangerie in Strasbourg in 1935 at the age of three. My father had just died.

My mother kept everything, and so did I. Nothing was thrown away. After my mother's death, I discovered a plastic bag full of her hair, picked from the comb before and during the war. What was she planning to do with it? Did she have in mind to knit a sweater for her darling son?

Mementos, letters, and documents of all kinds were hoarded. Thus, all of my early drawings, scrapbooks, schoolbooks and reports, and newspaper clippings remain as a testament to what I witnessed as a child. Thanks to this accumulation of material, I am able to recreate and chronicle those absurd and tragic times that were to mark my life to this day.

My father, Theo Ungerer, was born into a patrician family. With his brother, he ran a family-owned factory producing astronomical clocks. He was a true renaissance man: inventor, writer (in German, French and Alsatian), engineer, historian, painter, illustrator, and bibliophile. His curiosity knew no bounds; he was a pure aesthete, obsessed with beauty in nature and art.

Born in 1931, I was three years old when my father died in his native Strasbourg, leaving me, my mother Alice, my brother Bernard, and my two sisters Edith and Vivette behind. I was the youngest by ten years—an accident, according to my mother. The center of my world was my family, and as a seedling I was lucky to land on fertile ground. My talents were welcomed with enthusiasm at home, and I was constantly encouraged to draw and write by my mother, brother, and sisters.

Papa's absence filled me with sad frustration. I envied my brother and sisters for having known him. He became a mythical figure to me, still lingering in the library, peering out of his favorite collectables, ticking in every clock. He was constantly evoked by the family—the hero they knew, the one I would never meet.

After my christening, 1932, in our house in Strasbourg that my father designed, where I still live today.

The note below written by my mother says: "A lock of hair from our little darling Tomi, cut the evening before his first birthday." She wrote the month on the date incorrectly as September instead of November.

petite boucle blonde de notre tout petit chéri Tomy, coupée la veille de son premier anniversaire.
27. IX. 1932

Sometimes, when left alone, I would wind up the old brass music box made by my grandfather and listen. Crying away, I would watch the spiked cylinders unwind, plucking out the melody over and over. Papa was dead, yet the music seemed to summon his presence, like Aladdin's lamp. This music box, which I inherited, still remains a kind of telephone to the netherworld. Much later in life, I realized that when Papa died, he left me all of his talents, and I can still feel his presence, especially when I work.

When my father died, my mother was left indigent. We moved to Logelbach, an industrial suburb near Colmar. My grandfather had been the manager of the Haussmann textile factory, and my grandmother still lived there in a big building with four apartments. We moved into the empty apartment above my grandmother, below an enormous attic space with dormer windows overlooking the fields beyond on one side, the factory on the other.

Logelbach
The Henk, *workers' quarters*   *Administrative buildings*

PREMIÈRE ÉGLISE D'ALSACE
Style Art Moderne

LOGELBACH HAUT-RHIN

Standing amid the factory's chimneys, the unique white spire of the Logelbach church rose out of the distance like a minaret, giving our gray suburb the allure of an oasis. My mother considered it to be proof of Catholic bad taste—even worse than Art Nouveau, which she automatically dismissed as kitsch.

Our house—we lived upstairs, right

Prison camp

The Abbé Glory, my godfather Pam, my brother Bernard and Papa holding my hands, Mama, and my sisters Edith and Vivette.

With Papa in 1934.

We could have lived in relative prosperity, but the income from my father's share in the Ungerer clock factory was fully absorbed in paying the mortgage on the big villa in Strasbourg that he had designed and built before his death. Mama refused to sell it, and chose to rent it out and live on nothing in Logelbach.

The house in Logelbach had been designed to accommodate the managers of the factory. The front yard was lined with huge chestnut trees. Surrounding the house were large flower and vegetable gardens designed by my grandfather. A gravel path between trees—walnut, cherry, hazelnut, prune, pear, and mulberry—led to a *gloriette*, a gazebo covered with vines. The gardens were designed to provide ideal childhood memories. The house was adjacent to a beautiful park that surrounded a neo-gothic building of dark red sandstone that housed the local infirmary run by nuns in starched hats. Next to the building was the mortuary, a small chapel that filled me with awe. The park to which we had access had an alley of chestnut trees leading to the open fields. Across the street were the factory buildings, one empty—later to be used as a prison camp.

For food we depended on the big vegetable garden.

Most things were canned, peas and beans were dried. If a storm approached, we all knelt and prayed, Mama imploring the Lord to spare us from hail. As the big black clouds, like herds of *bêtes noires*, passed by, ignoring us, Mama with tears in her eyes would stand up and thank God for another miracle.

I remember the beautiful lilac bushes in the flower garden, not for their pungent smell that permeated the spring evenings, but because my mother sometimes dressed herself up as an old farm woman in order to sell bouquets of them—incognito—at the railroad station. The lilacs that my mother sold were the lilacs of despair and courage.

I was seven years old when the war broke out in 1939. At the time, I was going to school in Colmar, two miles away, at the Lycée Bartholdi, the proper school to go to in the area according to my mother. She did not want me to attend the local school for fear of the bad influence the local street urchins might have on me. Mama had what we call in Alsatian a *gratl.* She was very class conscious, imbued with Protestant and bourgeois values. With equal disdain, she frowned upon the working classes (rabble), Catholics, and nouveau riche.

My mother was a stunning beauty, and she had the greatest respect, bordering on awe, for nobility. I am sure that she would have given anything for a transfusion of blue blood into her veins. I even wonder what would have happened in her mind if the Fuhrer had been born "Hitler von Braunau" (Hitler was born in Braunau in Austria).

My favorite photograph of my father, 1934.

The brass music box crafted by my grandfather was my contact to the netherworld. With the microscope, I discovered the hidden wonders of nature.

At four years of age, next to a mullein plant. This herb inspired my mother's poem on the next page.

Facing:
My mother's beauty was frowned upon by her puritan relatives. According to the Bible, in their opinion, only whores wore make-up and dyed their hair.

Though penniless, Mama played her part of a lady with perfection. She was treated with the utmost respect by everyone in Logelbach. From the earliest age, I found this very embarrassing. When I was sent on an errand to the grocery shop, I never had to stand in line. Upon entering the shop, it became silent. The servile shopkeeper would always say, "and what can I do for the little boy of 'good family?'"

I remember the day when, sneaking below the glass on the top half of the grocer's door so as not to be seen, I stuffed a firecracker in the keyhole and ran away after the explosion with the merchant on my heels. He followed me all the way under the attic gables where I was trying to hide and, holding me by the earlobe, dragged me to my mother who promised him that I would be spanked for this prank. The moment he left, Mama shut the door convulsed in laughter, and took me in her arms and congratulated me with kisses—which was punishment of a kind, as I hated to be kissed. (Mama loved practical jokes. With great pride she told us how, when she was little, she had treated the ladies who visited her mother for tea every Thursday with rabbit droppings sprinkled with powdered sugar, and how, with pinched lips, they had asked Grandmother for the recipe.)

There was also the baker (later arrested by the Gestapo), and the butcher, where I seldom went, for meat was expensive and a luxury for us. He would give me a slice of salami, leaving me to ponder why the lower-class housewives could fill their shopping bags with meats and patés, while we, with our beautiful antiques, library, and objets d'art, had to live without the luxuries our well-born stomachs craved.

You proud mullein,
You magnificent candelabra,
Your gold fills my heart
And makes it laugh with joy.

Your flowering miracle
Renews itself each day.
I cheerfully pick it,
As well as I can,
For your stars are high up,
Up to the sky,
They beckon me from afar
To look at them.

I greet your giants
Of silver-green velvet,
From which the buds spray
Like gold from the hand of God.

You grow in wild soil,
Nourished by stone and sand;
Heaven is your breath,
The sun your gown!

Nature leaves itself from the
Dew in your goblet,
Nature's topers hum
A song in major and minor!

The bees return heavy laden
And sated with their feast
Back safely to the hive.

Thus will I too wander
   homeward
With my sweet burden,
And cook up for the others
What you have bestowed!

Farewell you lovely plant,
You light of the true light.
With your splendor you
Have sparked a poem
In which I want to tell you
How rich you have made me
With the miraculous gifts
Of your flowering splendor.

I thank you from my heart
For your fragrant sap
Whose balsam rids body
And soul of all aches and pains.

Alice Ungerer
(TRANSLATED BY BURT PIKE)

The house in Logelbach, drawn by my father in 1913 when he was courting my mother, Alice Essler.

My teddy bear.

My mother was born and raised in the house in Logelbach in the time of Kaiser Wilhelm, when Alsace was German. She had perfectly romantic recollections of those "good old times," which ended with the First World War, yet she always considered herself French—a patriot, a chauvinist, more French than the French. She was practically allergic to the Germans, but that didn't keep her from writing poetry in Goethe's language, and declaiming large excerpts from prose and poetry, as if on stage. She was infused with the poetry of the German Romantics. She wrote well (her French sometimes extravagant) and she also spoke Alsatian. There were poems for every occasion and she would often recite with tears in her eyes. A mountaintop view would evoke lines from Gottfried Keller: "Drink, oh my eyes, what my lashes hold, of the golden overflow of this world . . ."

(She left behind a trunk of poems, letters, and essays, in which I found a letter to Nixon, her hero at the time of the Watergate scandal. She had addressed him as *Fier et galant chevalier* (Proud and gallant knight).)

We had moved back into the house of my mother's youth to my grandmother's great surprise. Unbeknownst to her, Mama had obtained permission to use the apartment above Grandmama directly from the factory's director because of the years of faithful service my grandfather had put in as a manager of the factory. We surreptitiously moved in on a day my grandmother went to town for tea with her friends and were there when Grandmama returned. She threw a fit—to have a daughter with children so near! This was the end!

She would sit most of the day by the window in an alcove in her dining room. Her peace was continuously disrupted by my teddy bear. From the window above I would let him swing at the end of a string—his appearance drove her crazy. I would listen for the squeak of her window and watch for her white hand darting out in an attempt to catch the unfortunate beast. At the last possible moment I would quickly tug on the string and pull my furry accomplice out of her reach. The teddy bear was never caught—I still have it today. I don't remember her talking to me—I only remember her face flattened against the window pane, grimacing like a squashed ghost to frighten me. Her meanness was compensated for by the presence of my Aunt Suzanne who lived with her. She was a nurse, later to become a deaconess. She was a ray of sunshine, intelligent and modest. She took care of my cousin Andrée whose father, shell-shocked in the war, lived in an asylum.

My grandmother was very religious, and although Protestant, she was fascinated by the little St. Thérèse of Lisieux. My mother was the same, and called upon St. Anthony of Padua whenever she misplaced something.

My staunch Protestant grandmother worshipped St. Thérèse of Lisieux. She gave my mother this picture, when my father was in the hospital, with a note: "You have now been punished enough for your sins. It is time now to put this holy picture under the pillow of our dear Theo. And don't forget to pay me back the five francs it cost me."

9

A class picture of my first year in school. I am in the middle of the back row, behind the teacher.

Facing:
A drawing of Mickey Mouse that survived Uncle Heino's raids.

Proclaiming "*Oh quel miracle*," she would always find the lost object after invoking his name. Grandmama was an unpleasant woman and died shortly before the war of food poisoning from soup that had turned as sour as her character.

While I attended the Lycée Bartholdi, I boarded with my Aunt Marguerite whose husband Heino was an evangelist from Switzerland. They lived a few minutes from the Lycée. I only came home on weekends. They had a spaniel named Bouli that was a vegetarian, and a maid with the biblical name of Josepha. My uncle was a man whose puritanism was as blind as his faith. He was stern, his incredibly high forehead sheltering the Ten Commandments. He disapproved of my drawings—most of them caricatures—especially those inspired by Walt Disney. Since God had created man in his image, my pictures were sacrilegious. I woke up once in the middle of the night to the eerie sight of my uncle in his nightshirt, rummaging, and sneaking away with my sinful drawings. In his mind these incriminating documents had to be destroyed before doomsday, to spare me the evidence of my sins.

Bon Point

"Good Point" merit stubs were given to us at school. Ten of them could be traded for a picture.

Prise de Constantine (1837)

The picture that came with my first stick of chewing gum given to me by a classmate, shown here at actual size.

Facing:
A page from one of my first school copybooks. This patriotic poem glorifies the French flag that was soon to change colors. The illustration shows children in traditional Alsatian costumes, with two tricolor cocardes on the girl's hair knot.

Uncle Heino himself was afflicted by one of the deadly sins—gluttony! He loved sweets. For one of my birthdays, I was given a box of chocolates. I took one, passed the box around, and as I reached for a second one I was stopped and given a lesson on how sinful it was to indulge. Most of the chocolates set aside for safekeeping mysteriously disappeared.

Once I came home with a stick of chewing gum. As I was opening it my uncle intervened. "What is this and where did you get it?" He decided that it was his responsibility to sample this new product. This was possibly well meant since he might save my life—just as in the time of the Borgias the servants tasted the dishes of their masters in case they might be poisoned. Well, he did not know that chewing gum was made for chewing: he took the stick—two by two-and-a-half inches—swallowed it, and declared it tasteless and not fit for a child's consumption. I remember the size because a picture came with each stick, and we collected them as kids—I still have the picture of the French army conquering Constantine, Algeria, in 1837. I never found out what blocking effects this glob of gum had on his austere digestion.

One Sunday before church I found a plateful of hosts. Even though I didn't know what they were for, I ate them all. My uncle was devastated and explained to me that I had gorged myself on Jesus. I was not punished, but his making me feel guilty was worse than any punishment.

I must say that my uncle and aunt both took care of me as if I was their own child, with concern and their own brand of affection, but I was miserable and felt rejected by my family. In school I had no friends, my clothes were shabby, and I was shy if not terrified. On weekends one of my sisters would take me home on the back of her bicycle. There I would be drowned in a del-

Vive la France, vive la France, l'ot Isace et la Lor-
raine!

2eme couplet

Fier drapeau en avant
et la mode française
Vous suivons en chantant
La Marseillaise
Qu'il est joli, qu'il est beau
Ce petit cher drapeau

I was literally allergic to grammar and arithmetic, and it gave me great hope and inspiration to share the same talent as the boy pictured in one of my schoolbooks bearing the caption "young artist."

uge of my mother's kisses. I was her little *cheri*.

My mother's uncontrolled displays of affection were for me terribly annoying, especially in public, and the effusion of kisses—particularly the wet ones—revolted me. All of this, and a repertoire of endearing expressions: my sunshine, my little tiger, darling sparrow, little goldbug, *Meschtgräzerle* (little rooster scratching the dung pile), and worst of all, *Schisserle* (baby with his pants full of shit!). Even now, when I hear these words, I feel like crawling and hiding under the nearest table, which, as a matter of fact, I often did as a child—once during dinner with a bellow, pumping air under my aunt's skirt. "Alice, this room is very drafty," she complained to my mother.

I was a fully grown man of forty-five when, home for a visit, my mother took me in her arms and in front of family and friends said, "My prince, my fairy tale prince, look at you, how beautiful you look." Turning to the others, she added, "He is beautiful because he looks like me!" It is a fact, I look like my mother, and this has always bothered me. Why couldn't I resemble my father? It bothers me especially when I see myself on television or when I look at myself in the mirror, shaving. My nephew said, "Stop shaving! Then you won't have to look at yourself, and a beard might mar the resemblance!" That is probably why I grew a beard as soon as I could, in high school.

My brother Bernard was the head of the family. I shared a room with him when I was home, but I didn't see him often, as he was busy studying and giving private lessons. He was intelligent, hardworking, stern in his running of the family—he took his role seriously. His teachers all agreed he was the best pupil they ever had.

I was my sisters' toy. We had an illustrated edition of *Little Lord Fauntleroy* that turned out to be a source of inspiration to my sisters. With old bits of cloth and the help of the Singer sewing machine they created for me the "cutest" outfit, with puffed sleeves and lace. After curling my hair they deposited me at school the next morning. What for my mother and sisters was the most beguiling and charming ensemble provoked a unanimous uproar of jeers and catcalls from my schoolmates. I was the sissy of the class. I went blind with rage and kicked one boy in the knee, for which I was severely punished.

My sister Vivette had taught me to knit, so for her birthday I knitted her a sanitary napkin—in my innocence I didn't know what they were for, I only thought them useful because they were always hanging on the washline. And only much later did I find out the meaning of the expression, "a visit from Potsdam," which was a euphemism for menstruation—I couldn't understand why Mama and my sisters, hating the Germans as they did, should expect a visit from Prussia.

My sisters knew how to tease me. As I bent over my schoolwork they would sneak behind me and plant a kiss on my neck. One day in a blind rage I threw myself upon Vivette with clenched fists, kicking. She fell on the floor, lifeless. I was panic stricken—"I've killed my sister, my sister!" Sobbing, saying, "Forgive me!" I was shaking her by the shoulders when she suddenly sat up, opened her eyes, and exploded into a mocking peal of laughter.

When begging for a little understanding I would say, "*Toi tu n'est pas moi*" (You are not me), and the whole family would repeat in unison "*toitunestpasmoi*." I was the youngest, never taken seriously. And always, I couldn't

Our family's favorite summer resort was the Hohrodberg in the Vosges mountains. The area was still scarred by the trenches of the First World War. Strewn with bunkers and littered with helmets and arms, it was an ideal playground for me and my brother.

The cover of Le Journal de Mickey *stuffed with Walt Disney comics later declared degenerate by the Nazis.*

understand: If Mama loves me, why does she send me away? Life was already full of contradictions.

Old friends of my father's sometimes came to visit, like the Abbé Glory, with whom Papa had written a book. He was one of the most distinguished speleologists of his time. I met him again after the war and took part in one of his expeditions underground. A small fat Frenchman, he nevertheless could crawl through crevasses with great agility.

My godfather, Pam, was in the French navy. He came whenever he was on leave to spoil me with presents. I remember him skipping a ten-franc coin (the size of a silver dollar) over a pond. There were plenty of uncles and aunts. Aunt Loulou, my mother's younger sister, was married to a country doctor, Uncle Freddy. I occasionally stayed with them during the summer and spent wonderful holidays there. They had the first cat I had ever seen, and one day I pushed it from the second-floor window and it landed on its feet unharmed. When it had kittens, my cousin Maurice was told to dispose of them, and he brought me along as a witness. One by one he hurled them against a wall, like snowballs, and they fell lifeless to the ground like empty satchels. This was my first experience of death through violence, a foretaste of what the Nazis were to inflict upon the Alsatians.

Life was peaceful, despite the fact that my mother carried on a feud with our neighbors, the Backs, who lived across from us on the same floor. Mr. Back was the accountant for the Haussmann factory, a decent, quiet man who could also explode in terrible fits of rage, as I found out one day when black shoe polish I had smeared on the handrail of the staircase found its way onto his coat sleeve. He screamed at my mother, waving the soiled sleeve in her face. After he left, and our door was closed, Mama praised me for my ingenuity.

Mama considered the Backs vulgar, and thus unworthy of living in the same building. She called Mrs. Back "that Back woman." They had a son who was studying to be a pharmacist and who later became quite famous as the director of the laboratory at the Pasteur Institute in Colmar. This tall, reserved young man left a copy of Walt Disney's magazine *Mickey* for me on our doorstep every Saturday morning. His kind gesture has remained for me an important life lesson—to see goodwill as a rainbow bridging two storms. It left me wondering about the nature of grudges, and the arrogance of a privileged class toward people who were different. Then and there my loathing for class prejudice started to grow.

My brother was a Boy Scout. I admired his uniform and envied the chocolate bar my mother gave him for his outings.

My gas mask and the metal container that it came with. Everyone was provided with one and required to carry it to school or work.

An illustration from the instructions for putting on the gas mask.

War was declared in September 1939. My Uncle Heino was called back by his church to his native Switzerland. I was boarded with another pastor who had a son my age, Christian, and for the first time I discovered the fun of having someone to play with.

Gas masks were distributed and compulsory—we were made to carry them everywhere in grey cylinders. Breathing through them gave you the impression of having rubber lungs. There was fear and dread in the air. Our greatest fear was of evacuation. France's border ran along the Rhine and was protected by the Maginot Line. The French government, worried about the welfare of the people, decided to evacuate all inhabitants in a strip of land, three miles wide, along the Rhine. On September 1, 1939, three hundred and eighty thousand Alsatians, of which one hundred thousand were in Strasbourg, were ordered to pack a suitcase, a blanket, and enough food for four days within twenty-four hours. In trains, sometimes in cattle wagons, they were moved to the southwest of France. There they were not exactly welcome, especially because most of them had German accents and spoke little French.

Strasbourg was an empty city. Winter came and all the plumbing froze. The entire university was moved to Clermont-Ferrand; libraries and the contents of the museum were shipped away. The farms in this no man's land were abandoned overnight with unmilked cows mooing over their bursting udders. We were on the alert for being evacuated as well, ready with packed suitcases. In my rucksack was my teddy bear (my best friend) wearing my old white striped pants that I had outgrown. One afternoon I returned home to find that my mother wasn't there. I was seized with a sickening panic that she might have been evacuated without me, but she returned from her errand and all was well again.

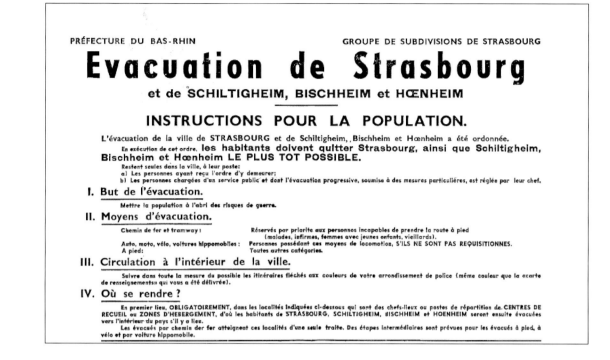

Part of the order to evacuate Strasbourg and a strip of land three miles wide along the Rhine. It was posted in French and German. 380,000 Alsatians were given 24 hours to pack 30 kg of luggage, enough food for four days, a blanket, fork, spoon, knife, cup, one pair of shoes, etc. They were shipped in convoys to the south of France. All non-French citizens had to report to the police.

Stray cats in the deserted streets of Strasbourg after the French government ordered its evacuation.

Was it after the French officers got me drunk that I cut this ad out of a magazine, or was I attracted to the uniforms of the Allies? The caption reads: "In 1940: the French and English armies drink Chartreuse in the officers' clubs, on tables in the mess, and from flasks carried in the soldiers' packs."

The French government ordered the public schools to be closed. I was sent to the College St. André, which was privately run by the Catholic Church. As a Protestant I was dismissed from morning mass. Once, clowning around, performing a balancing act between two desks, I slipped and fell on my head, resulting in a fractured skull, which later turned out to be a blessing in disguise. I passed out, and as I came to my senses I asked, "Where am I?" I knew very well where I was, but I had read this line in a story and was now using it to impress my teacher. Was I already as good an actor as my mother, delivering the right line at the right moment?

The French army was everywhere. My grandmother's apartment, empty since her death, was requisitioned. Officers moved in with their own cooks. It was obvious that pots and pans were more important for winning the war than guns and cannons. These officers, still on horses, invited me one day to sample an array of *apéritifs*,

The cover of the popular French magazine Marie Claire *at the time of the German invasion. Insouciance prevailed in the French Press, flippant as ever: "We shall win, so what!"*

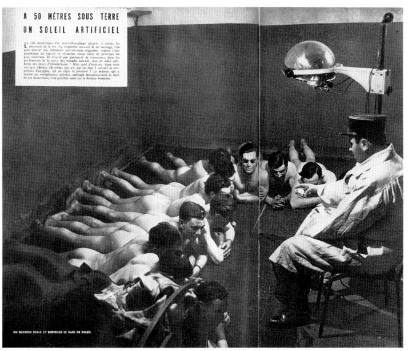

Down below, inside the Maginot Line, in a beachlike atmosphere, these French soldiers are offering their backsides to sunlamps, getting ready for the German tanning.

The troops were served coffee laced with bromide to squelch their sexual urges.

Passionnément

Tout bouillonne et s'agite en mon être troublé.
Le délire est en moi, mais mon cœur est charmé.

316

Passionnément

J'aime ta chair exquise et son parfum troublant
Et mon cœur, malgré moi, bat d'un rythme violent.

316

Passionnément

Tes lèvres sont pour moi comme un fruit savoureux
Qui enchante, qui grise et rend mon cœur heureux.

316

digestifs, and *eau de vies* (spirits). Later my mother found me passed out on our doorstep. She thought I was dead—not so farfetched since I was born with a heart defect and rheumatic fever.

At home alcohol was frowned upon—no wine, no beer, only schnapps, which was used medicinally to treat indigestion or colds and disinfect wounds. Mama's older brother Uncle Henri was an alcoholic who lived in sin with a woman I never met. He was a geologist who dabbled in chemistry (during the war he discovered a way to produce sugar out of malt). Before the First World War he was in German East Africa (now Namibia) and had discovered copper deposits in the desert. Alsatians being German at the time, he happily spent the war as a prisoner of the English. There were still crates of Uncle Henri's minerals and African trophies in our attic. It was there, pondering over blocks of malachite and azurite, that I developed my penchant for geology and mineralogy. Later as an amateur at the age of seventeen, I discovered the first deposits of uranium in Alsace.

Uncle Henri was the black sheep of the family. "Don't ever drink or you will turn out like him." Many years later, when I would take Mama to restaurants, to partake with friends of my enjoyment of life, she would anxiously watch my preference for empty bottles. Each time I would look away she would empty my glass, thinking that she would reduce my intake, not realizing that an empty bottle can always be replaced by a full one. To what amount of self-sacrifice can mothers be driven to save their sons? In the end she was the tipsy one, singing, praising the Lord with hymns on the way home— "Onward, Christian soldiers. . . ."

With my fractured skull I was not allowed to run or exercise. I had more time to read, to putter around and draw. My sister Vivette at the time worked at the gov-

The famous bidon *designed to carry wine for the* poilu *(French soldiers) carried during World War I. It was still believed in 1939–1940 that wine was the fuel to victory. (Poilu meant unshaven. As there was no water for this luxury in the trenches, many soldiers let their beards grow.)*

ernment prefecture and all my drawings of this period were made on the backs of formulas and certificates of military allocations.

War meant shortages. We lived from the garden, and our less than modest income hadn't made us major consumers. But still, with sugar, oil, coffee, and other staples being rationed, there was already a problem, although these shortages didn't affect the valiant officers wallowing in their unbuttoned uniforms below.

I was drawing, among other subjects, cross-sections of houses with stores of food—everyone was now hoarding. One room was shelved from floor to ceiling with just sardine tins! There were larders full of hams and smoked sausages, sacks of sugar and barrels of olive oil. Olive oil was a luxury—although the French army cooks had plenty. The first olive oil I ever tasted dates from the time Mama traded a kiss with the officer's chef for a bottle of it. She bragged about it: "Oh, isn't it wonderful—a liter of olive oil for one kiss!" My mother knew how to use her beauty as live bait—she would lure, tantalize, get what she wanted, but nobody could touch her.

French propaganda taught us to fear the barbaric Huns who cut off children's hands.

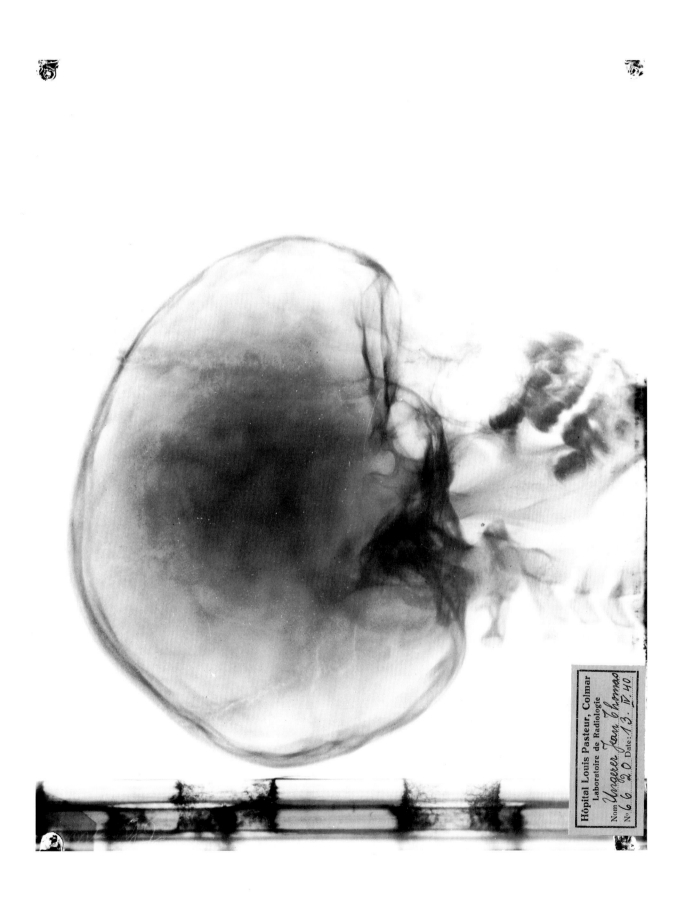

BONS d'ARMEMENT

Mon papa a souscrit...
et le tien?

7

Vous trouverez tous les détails qui vous intéressent sur les Bons d'Armement dans la brochure gratuite éditée par le Ministère des Finances. Pour la recevoir, sans aucun engagement de votre part, remplissez et découpez le coupon ci-contre et adressez-le au Ministère des Finances, Service B , r. de Rivoli, Paris

Nom ....
Profession .... Age ....
Adresse ....

La drôle de guerre—how can I translate this? The funny war, the odd war. *Sitzkrieg*, the German equivalent, is easier to translate: the sitting war. I would call it the loafing war. The French were totally vain about their absolute superiority—"We have the Maginot Line." "*Ils ne passeront pas*" (They will not pass). Impregnable, there was no reason to keep fit or on the ready. All we had to do was wait and show them that we were there.

Every officer was a crowing rooster in this gallinaceous army. Lax, unkempt, sometimes unshaven, they nonchalantly hung around. Some still wore the blue uniform dating back to the First World War. I do not remember ever seeing them march, exercise or train. Fashionably smoking pipes, humming the latest hit song—"I shall wait, day and night I shall wait forever"—little did they know the waiting would last four years, and behind wires as barbed as their unshaven jowls like stalactites formed from a trickle of boredom.

Sitzkrieg. A clipping out of Paris Match *showing a valiant French soldier in action daring the Germans to cross the Rhine.*

Regimental insignia of the French soldiers stationed on the Maginot Line.

Blitzkrieg. *Hansi, the Alsatian author and illustrator, hated the Teutons, as evidenced in his cartoon of these Wagnerian Germans looking over the Rhine toward Alsace. In his* History of Alsace Told for Young Children, *he systematically instilled hatred of the Germans with a talent that inspired me. He was the artist who exerted the greatest influence on me as a child.*

And for me, what were the Germans? I would have been totally terrified had I not been convinced of French infallibility. "We shall win, because we are the strongest." I had been completely brainwashed in school and at home. I was blinded with patriotism, filled with the sparkling deeds of French heroes. And, of course, the French were all good, the Germans all bad, and the rest of the world not as bad. I remember that I was worried about my hands—I had heard in school that the Germans would come and chop off the hands of all the children. This fabrication went back to World War I when some children in Belgium were maimed playing with hand grenades.

I was brought up with the books of Hansi, a talented Alsatian illustrator and writer. His *History of Alsace Told for Young Children* was a twisted rewrite of history, the work of a bigot who insidiously and systematically taught us to hate our neighbors. His picture of the Huns waiting across the Rhine reminds me of a satirical song sung during the Nazi times:

> The ancient Germans they sat
> On both banks of the Rhine,
> Sitting on bearskins
> And guzzling their mead.
> Till one day appeared
> A Roman with a friendly hello
> "Heil Hitler!" he hailed,
> My name is Ta(ha)citus!

The arrival of the Wehrmacht, *the German Army, as I saw it in 1940.*

The Germans didn't just arrive, they marched in. Imagine my surprise—I was standing in the front yard when a motorcycle with a sidecar drove by. I had a toy pistol in my hand, which I threw to the ground for fear of being taken for a partisan. It was the 17th of June, 1940, around noon, and the air was silent with heat. I heard them first, the cadenced beat of their marching, and then I saw them—the first infantry units, with real boots on their feet, real rucksacks on their backs, real guns on their shoulders. The regiment was ordered to stop in front of our house. The guns were propped

This is exactly how I remember the German army—marching and singing. You could hear them coming from a distance, pounding the ground on hobnailed boots. Later, in Russia, the soldiers' feet would freeze because the metallic nails conducted the extreme cold inside their boots.

upright neatly in pyramids of three while the unit of young smiling faces broke out, laughing and joking.

A horse-drawn field kitchen pulled up, and lunch was served. Fascinated, I went out on the sidewalk, and a beaming soldier offered me a taste of his soup. Then they marched on. They were not the hordes of Huns I had so vividly imagined, and what's more, they seemed nice, even cordial. I had just tripped over another question mark!

Thus, the Germans entered Alsace. Crack units on rubber rafts crossed the Rhine as the Maginot Line

As all metal was needed for the war effort, this highly realistic miniature German soldier was made from elastolin, a type of plastic.

My drawing of German soldiers lining up at the field kitchen.

This scene is very much like the one in front of our house in Logelbach the day the first troops arrived.

turned out to be useless. The operation was swift—the French troops stationed with us vanished overnight without putting up a fight—and, not facing any resistance, the German troops marched in.

In neighboring Colmar, *Oberst* Koch, commander of the crack "Adolf Hitler" unit, ordered immediate delivery of 2300 kg of bread, 557 kg of sausages, 290 kg of butter, 7 kg of tea, 23 kg of coffee, 290 liters of rum, and 23,000 packs of cigarettes; on top of that, twenty hostages, preferably Francophile civil servants. I guess they brought their own potatoes, but no wine! This would have been a French priority. The soldiers behaved well, and like good customers, emptied the shops. The French franc was devalued to five pfennigs. For them, it was paradise on earth, and they lived it up like *Gott in Frankreich* (God in France).

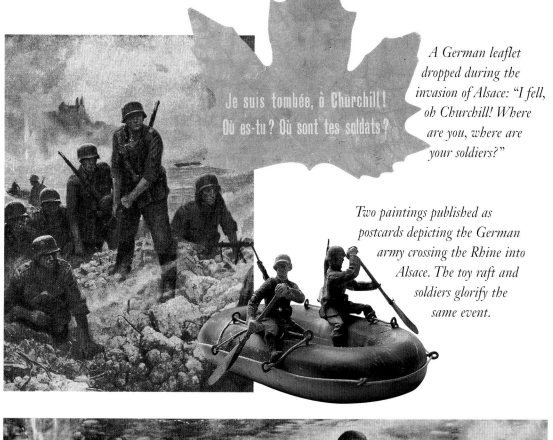

Je suis tombée, ò Churchill !
Où es-tu ? Où sont tes soldats ?

A German leaflet dropped during the invasion of Alsace: "I fell, oh Churchill! Where are you, where are your soldiers?"

Two paintings published as postcards depicting the German army crossing the Rhine into Alsace. The toy raft and soldiers glorify the same event.

Trinken, trinken das hab ich gern
Bier , Bier vom Flasche in dem Bauer
es ist gutes ist gut , trinken trinken

Facing:
Your friendly neighbor is here! The image of the German soldier in propaganda was totally different from the way I drew them. They were both studies in extremes.

I made these two drawings of German soldiers according to Hansi and not from reality. Left, the caption reads: "Drinking, Drinking, I love it a lot. Beer, Beer, from bottle to stomach, it is good to drink, drink." The caption for the drawing below reads: "This one came back from Alsace not with an Iron Cross but a big fat belly."

On the 16th of July all Jews who remained in Alsace were told that they had twenty-four hours to pack a suitcase and enough food for five days. They were allowed 2,000 francs per person, but gold, jewelry, and wedding rings were to be left behind.

After the arrival of the Nazis, Alsace was, as far I know, the only place where Jews were not crowded into ghettos. They were simply deported to France in convoys. Later they were to be hunted down, arrested, and delivered to the Gestapo by the French. The French from the interior (*de l'interieur* as we called them in Alsace), and all *Volksfeindlich* (enemies of the people) were sent back to France under similar circumstances. Within six months Colmar was to lose one-third of its population, while shops, houses, furniture, and all assets were confiscated.

Der da ist von Elsaß zurück gekommen nich mit Ritterkreuz mit einem aber dick Bauer

This old postcard was sent to my mother by a young German admirer in uniform during World War I. He came to visit her again in 1940, as a general in the Wehrmacht. *(Facing) This figurine of an officer looks exactly like him.*

There was no housing shortage and plenty of accommodations for the Germans who moved in to administer us and oversee the functioning of the "new order." They arrived like tourists stepping off a tour bus.

About a week after the Nazis' arrival, an enormous chauffeur-driven Mercedes stopped and entered our yard. A tall, good-looking officer with a broad, decorated chest stepped out—the nearest thing to Curt Jurgens, the movie star. He walked up, rang the bell, and my mother opened the door.

"*Meine Liebe Alice!*" Mama turned to stone—what would the neighbors think? He was an old friend from her youth, an era of long skirts, huge hats, and parasols, and he had not forgotten the wonderful times spent in the *Drei Mäderl Haus* (the house of the three young girls in the Haussmannstrasse). Thank God he was only making a detour and wasn't staying. He gave me a bar of chocolate, promising me that after the great and final victory I'd have all the chocolate I could eat. And this for a thousand years to come! Heil Hitler!

What a debacle! Thousands and thousands of French soldiers were taken prisoner. They were herded—sweating in their woolen uniforms, haggard and dejected—down to the huge old factory building across the street that was now a prison camp. With the rest of the population we literally passed buckets of water to sooth their thirst, and gave them food. The German guards, content and smiling, let us distribute all we wanted, not knowing that four years later they would follow the same path.

These prisoners, who a few weeks before had been strutting and crowing, were now deflated, disposed of like old socks. Heaps of their helmets, useless now, were thrown into the nearby gravel pits. I had a whole collection of them, all heavily permeated with the smell of leather and sweat. This spectacle of defeat, more than the violence later on, convinced me that life wasn't worth such an absurdity.

The Alsatians earlier evacuated by the French government returned after the armistice in 1940. The Nazi propaganda machine exploited the return of this population "torn from the Reich" to the hilt. These poor people were stunned to be welcomed by fanfares and speeches by S.S. and S.A. officials, in a flurry of swastika flags. They had also returned to find that the French had needlessly blown the gas and electricity works to bits, as well as many bridges, as they retreated.

Thousands of French helmets were dumped in a nearby gravel pit.

The chestnut trees behind our house in Logelbach were still there when I took this photograph thirty years after the war.

The French officers who had been quartered in the apartment below us were gone now, leaving it free to be occupied by German officers. One day the doorbell rang. A German officer stood by the door, perfectly polite. He clicked his heels, took a bow, raised his arm and said, "*Heil Hitler.*" This was the first time (alas, not the last) that I heard that expression. He presented himself and, with the exaggerated smile of a fanatic, announced that he had three sons, two of them had already died for the Fuhrer, and he hoped the third one might be up to his brothers' example for the eternal glory of the Third Reich. Then, his face ecstatically Wagnerian, he declared, looking out at the row of chestnut trees: "Are they not beautiful at this time of the year? One thing I promise you: the day will come when you will see a Jew hanging from every branch." Then he pulled out a piece of paper. "This is a wonderful recipe for carrot cake. My wife gave it to me—it is yours." I witnessed this, but as I could not understand German yet, I give my mother's version of this event.

The situation took sharp turns daily. German was immediately proclaimed the official language. The common people spoke Alsatian, a German dialect, and had no trouble switching. But I, from a bourgeois background, spoke only French. My brother gave me a crash course, allowing me, three months later, to return to school. He performed wonders, using German translations of Kipling's *Jungle Books* and James Fenimore Cooper's *The Last of the Mohicans*. How quickly you can learn if you have to survive!

Hansi had suffered as a child under the Kaiser's educational system. I can't say that I identified with it either. (Note: the writing on the blackboard says "Berlin is the biggest city in the world.")

It was now obligatory for children to be sent to the local school. All Alsatian teachers were sent to Germany for *Umschulung* (recycling). They had to learn how to put the new system into practice and instill German pride and glory. They were replaced by young teachers, some in *Wehrmacht* uniforms (who had already served in Poland) and some in short Bavarian lederhosen—they were easy-going "missionaries." In every class hung a portrait of the Fuhrer, and every room was fitted with a *Volksender*, the word used for radio, on which we listened to Adolf Hitler every time he spoke. A whole new world was displaying its paraphernalia.

To my mother's dismay I had contact with the local kids for the first time in my life, able to play and make friends with all the *Wackes* (scamps). I was not rejected, but welcomed, if still an object of curiosity. Anyway, as the teacher said, we are all equal in the eyes of the Fuhrer and all blessed to be part of the great German Reich.

Once, though, I did get into a fight with another boy to prevent him from pulling the wings off a fly. I had been brought up to respect nature and all living things. With a blade of grass I would rescue insects from drowning in a puddle. However, this didn't stop me from squashing mosquitoes, catching flies and putting them in a miniature cage (made from two slices of a wine cork separated by bars made of needles), or keeping June bugs in matchboxes and letting them out during class.

Our new teachers, some in lederhosen, were of a different caliber than those portrayed by Hansi. Note the teacher's acknowledgment of the "Sieg Heil" from the Hitler Youth, while the Alsatian boy thumbs his nose in derision from behind.

My first assignment in school under the Nazis was to draw a Jew.

un juif

An illustration from a pre-war anti-Semitic postcard from Alsace directed personally at a Jewish merchant of Polish origins.

One of my first homework assignments was to draw a Jew. I came home and asked, "Mama, what is a Jew?" She said, "A Jew? Why?" "I have to draw one." "Well then, I think they want you to draw a man wearing glasses, with dark hair, a big nose, thick lips, and smoking a cigar." At school the depiction of Jews was so exaggerated that for us they seemed like fairy tale figures dragging huge sacks of gold. We lived in an industrial suburb, and no Jews lived in our neighborhood, although in most other towns or villages it was quite different.

Many years later, in 1956, I landed in New York with sixty dollars in my pocket and two trunks of drawings and manuscripts. In this huge mecca of magazines, publishers, and advertising agencies I was welcomed warmheartedly by the Jewish Americans that I met. Invited into their homes and even to Bar Mitzvahs, I was made to feel like one of the family. Most importantly, I discovered these new friends were like me and my family, not the caricatures portrayed in Nazi schoolbooks.

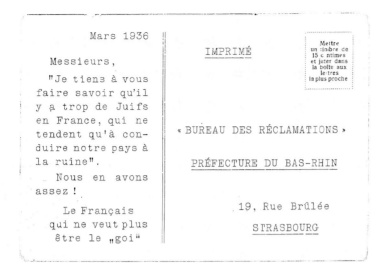

A pre-war anti-Semitic postcard printed in Strasbourg in 1936. It is addressed to the complaints department of the prefecture, and the message reads: "This is to let you know that there are too many Jews in France leading our country to ruin. Enough of this! The French don't want to be 'goys' any more."

- Je n'ai pas participé à la renaissance de la France, moi ? et tout ça, alors !..»

A French anti-Semitic drawing.

Hautes finances internationales.

Anti-Semitic propaganda was not just a German specialty. This picture was of French Vichy origin.

The French Revolution gave French Jews the right to be citizens. At the time eighty percent of the Jews in France lived in Alsace. Today the Jewish community in Strasbourg is the second largest in France after Paris. Strasbourg has seven synagogues, and is the seat of Radio Judaica, the only radio station of its kind in Europe.

The Jews are an intrinsic part of Alsatian culture, identity, and tradition, including gastronomy. Once I gave a speech at the main synagogue in Strasbourg and said: "Alsace has been sold to the Germans. Alsace has been sold to the French. It should have been sold to the Jews, then it would have stayed in the family." Alsatian Jews have specific genealogical trees. Names like Dreyfuss, Strauss, Katz, and Marx were common Jewish names in Alsace. The Yiddish and Alsatian dialects are very closely related, and Alsatian literature has been greatly enriched by the works of Jewish poets and others writers like Nathan Katz and, at present, Claude Vigée, who lives in Alsace and Israel.

Alsatian humor, which is the humor of a minority people, is closely linked to Jewish humor. As I always say, scratch an Alsatian and you'll find a Jew, and vice versa. Jewish and non-Jewish Alsatians have a lot in common. We are survivors, and as minorities within a large European state, we are very much attuned to each other.

We Alsatians take pride in our Jewish community. And when we say *Unseri Jüdde* (Our Jews), it means "one of us," that they are a part of us. When there is a sudden silence in the conversation, the French say, *Un ange qui passe* (An angel is passing by). The Alsatians say, "Psst, a Jew is entering paradise" (*a jüa kommt en Paradis*).

At the same time, anti-Semitism has existed in Alsace, like everywhere else, as evidenced by these post-cards printed before the Second World War. In the Middle Ages the Jews were occasionally persecuted and burned on pyres, and blamed for the Black Plague. The Nazis brought their own virulent brand of anti-Semitism to Alsace; it left with them when they were driven from our homeland by the Allies.

Willy Fischer, although older than me, was one of my best friends growing up. Like many Alsatians he was forced into the S.S., deserted, and went into hiding. His lifelong shame was to bear on his arm the S.S. tattoo. He detested the Germans, and would never let one into his home. Once I came to visit him with Percy Adlon (the German director of *Baghdad Cafe*) while he was making a film about me.

"No, no Krauts in here!"

"But Willy, he is half Jewish!"

"Then let the Jewish half come in, and the German half can stay out!"

Here you can already see the effects of German propaganda on me in 1940. My drawing shows a German soldier driving Uncle Sam and the Jewish-Anglo Americans out of the Reich.

The cover of the Nazi-published anti-Semitic book The Jewish Question in Education, *which contained guidelines for teachers on how to instruct their pupils in the "identification" of Jews so that they could be reported to the authorities.*

The anti-Semitic logo from the back cover of The Jewish Question in Education. *The caption reads: "Without a solution to the Jewish problem, there will be no redemption for humanity."*

An interior spread from a section of The Jewish Question in Education *that was a type of field guide for identification of Jews based on stereotypes. This page compares faces of "Aryan" and Jewish children. The following excerpts are translations of portions of the text. "The Jews have different noses, ears, lips, chins and different faces than Germans . . ." "They walk differently, have flat feet . . . their arms are longer and they speak differently . . ." "The teacher will have his pupils register these remarks in their 'Jew notebooks' . . . children educated with race discernment will be able, on first glance, to tell a Jew in a crowd of thousands."*

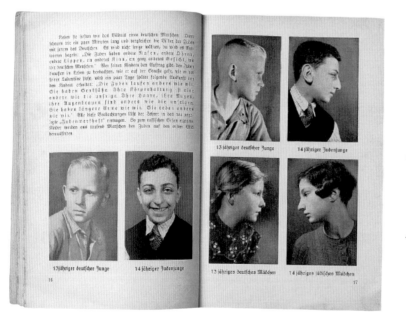

An illustration from The Jewish Question in Education *showing a child's depiction of a penniless Jew arriving in Germany from Palestine in 1918, and as a rich man in 1935.*

Anti-Semitic text from Hitler's Mein Kampf, *printed on high-quality paper for framing and displaying in the home.*

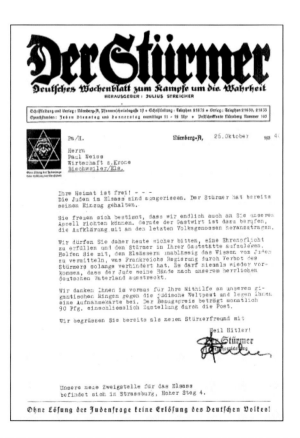

Letter from Der Sturmer, *the weekly paper that "fights for the truth," edited and published by Julius Streicher, pressuring a local restaurant owner to take a subscription. It is implied that if he doesn't take a subscription, he will be "on their list." The letter uses the same anti-Semitic slogan as the back cover of* The Jewish Question in Education. *Some of the text from the letter: "Your homeland is free. The Jews have been driven from Alsace . . . We take this opportunity to ask you to perform the honored duty of taking a subscription and displaying* Der Sturmer *in your restaurant."*

Seine Beute

Wie diese Ehe zustande kam, kann man sich denken, sie: eine hungrige Novize, er: der saturierte
Schlagerdichter, der sich mit genießerischer Bedachtsamkeit sein blondes Glück gekauft hat.

Man kann sich nicht genug darüber wundern, daß es die über die ganze Welt verstreute jüdische Nation versteht, ohne hörbares Kommando gleichmäßig linksum oder rechtsum zu schwenken. Was Rasse ist, weiß Juda schon seit Adam. Und Rassenschande haben die Hebräer für ihr Leben gern geübt. Das ging so weit, daß die tatkräftigen Rassenpropheten

Fascism was rampant within the German immigrant community in the U.S. in the late 1930s. Here is the cover of an edition of Junges Volk, *the magazine of the Young German-American Peoples Union, comparing Nazi martyr Horst Wessel to Lincoln. The caption says that they "both died for their country."*

The cover and inside page from an anti-Semitic Nazi booklet on the Jews in America. The sausage-eating man on the cover is none other than Mayor La Guardia of New York, an Italian American!

The Nazification of Alsace began immediately under the guise of *Aktion Elsass* (Action Alsace). The newly appointed governor of Alsace, *Gauleiter* Wagner, who was fully empowered by the Fuhrer, was responsible for implementing this program. It had all been well planned in advance, for upon the arrival of the Germans we were given schoolbooks and pamphlets specially conceived for Alsatian children. Posters were plastered everywhere with the slogan: "Away with the Gallic Trash." Every day the town crier announced new regulations from his bicycle, while decrees were showered upon us. The French past had to be systematically rooted out down to the smallest details, fringed with absurdities.

First, all names of French or foreign origins had to be translated or changed into German ones. Tomi was out and my real name, Jean Thomas, became Johann, or Hans. Somehow, through some kind of loophole, my sister Edith was able to hold on to her original name. Family names had to be changed as well: Grandjean became Grosshaus, Boulanger became Becker, Meunier became Muller, and so on.

Every family was given an *Ahnenpass*, a kind of passport with one's family tree going back four generations, "proving" that no Jewish blood had soiled our "Aryan" blood.

The names of all streets were changed—immediately all main streets became Adolf Hitler Strasse. In Strasbourg, Rue Chopin (a Pole) was replaced by Haydenstrasse (a German). In Mulhouse the main artery was called Rue du Sauvage (Street of the Savage); ironically the savage turned out to be Adolf Hitler. The French did the same thing when their chance came. There is an ongoing joke about these constant name changes: In 1871 an Alsatian in French was called *le garde* (guard), while in German he became *Wache* (guard). After 1918, the French came back and renamed him *vache* (cow),

Hitler in front of Strasbourg Cathedral in 1940.

Gauleiter *Robert Wagner (standing on left), the governor of Alsace,*
among a group of children in Strasbourg.

Wagner reviewing the troops at
the Nazi rally in Strasbourg on
October 12, 1941.

S.A. troops march through the streets of Wissembourg, October 19, 1941.

A Nazi rally in Colmar, September 28, 1941. A large group of Hitler youth drummers and musicians can be seen next to the nurses in the foreground. Note the white columns adorned with swastikas that I mention in the text.

*A mass Nazi rally in Strasbourg on October 12, 1941 in the Place Brolglie,
renamed Karl Roos Platz by the Germans after a Nazi martyr.*

*A march of 15,000
Nazis through the
streets of Strasbourg,
October 12, 1941.*

followed by the Germans in 1940 who said *Kuh* (cow).
Finally, once and for all, the French returned and
changed his name to *cul* (ass).

Germanization was especially difficult for the *Welsh*,
the name given to the inhabitants of the Vosges (a moun-
tainous area in France on the western side of Alsace)
because they spoke an ancient Romanic language. The
same applied to the names of localities. Alsatian village
names were literally unpronounceable by the French,
creating puddles of confusion reflecting the problematic
nature of our identity. For instance, today Rapschwihr in
Alsatian is Ribeauville in French and Rappoltsweiler in
German, and the French have great difficulties dealing
with untranslatable names of villages like Mittel-
schafholzheim (middle-sheep-wood-home).

Colmar was, and remains, a very chauvinistic town. I
always say that they are such patriots that they swallow a
tricolor *cocarde* (a folded patriotic ribbon) before meals to
be sure to digest in French. The inhabitants of the Rue
Goethe signed a petition after the war to replace the

My Hansi-inspired imaginary scene of the Germans sacking Alsace. The actual plundering was much more discreet.

name of their street and the municipality agreed. Why? Goethe was German.

The old monuments, which had been spared under the Kaiser, were all dismantled. Alsace had given the French Revolution and Napoleon many generals, some of whom were commemorated by bronze statues that were now pulled down and recycled for the German war effort. Some of these statues had been conceived by Bartholdi, the Colmar sculptor who designed the Statue of Liberty. The war memorial erected by the French in Strasbourg was spared; it shows a mourning woman with her two dead sons who died for France and for Germany—it is surprising that the Nazis didn't hack out the one who died for France. Every town and village had its memorial commemorating the dead who had fallen under various uniforms. There as well, the plaques were changed, and all the people who died for France suddenly died for Germany.

The French beret was a Gallic symbol, and it was

> **Verordnung**
> **über das Tragen der Franzosenmützen im Elsaß**
> **vom 13. Dezember 1941**
>
> **§ 1**
>
> Das Tragen von Franzosenmützen (Baskenmützen) im Elsaß ist verboten; unter das Verbot fallen auch solche Mützen, die den Franzosenmützen (Baskenmützen) nach Zuschnitt und Aussehen ähnlich sind.
>
> **§ 2**
>
> Es ist verboten, im Elsaß Mützen der in § 1 bezeichneten Art herzustellen oder zum Verkauf anzubieten oder solche Mützen in das Elsaß einzuführen.
>
> **§ 3**
>
> Zuwiderhandlungen gegen die §§ 1 und 2 werden mit Geldstrafen bis zu 150,— *RM* oder mit Haft bis zu 6 Wochen bestraft; die den Verboten der §§ 1 und 2 zuwider getragenen, hergestellten, zum Verkauf angebotenen oder eingeführten Mützen unterliegen der Einziehung.

The decree issued in Alsace on December 18, 1941 forbidding the wearing of berets.

forbidden to wear one. Renamed *Hirnverdunkelungskappe* (cap that obscures the forehead), you were punished with a fine of 150 Reichmarks and six months in prison if caught wearing one. This applied to Alsace only; in Germany a few miles away across the Rhine you could wear a beret without being punished. Some parents turned this into a joke and sent their children to school wearing absurd headgear, a real carnival!

Wedding rings had to be worn on the right hand, as was the custom in Germany. Bathroom faucets marked *chaud* or *froid* had to be replaced, as well as salt and pepper shakers.

It was forbidden to own any French books. We children were given wagons to go from house to house and collect them for burning, a joke because everyone simply hid them in boxes, and all we collected were old papers and magazines. You had to obtain official permission to

I cannot say now if this picture was inspired by stories of what happened in Poland, Russia, and elsewhere. One thing we knew: one act of open sabotage and this would happen to us.

consult a French dictionary, and any pictures with French captions and French diplomas were forbidden and had to go.

In Mulhouse there was a manufacturer of thermometers. The alcohol in the glass tube was red, the background white against a blue frame. The Germans ordered the colors changed and all old models surrendered. In cemeteries, all wreaths made of glass beads and wire in the French tradition were eliminated.

The use of French was strictly forbidden. A simple *Bonjour* or *Merci* was first punished by a fine and, later, immediate arrest and a jail sentence.

We were given Nazi armbands. I never wore mine, nor, to my knowledge, did anyone else.

Every sidestep was punishable and the word for concentration camp was clearly used in posters as a menace. There was a camp in Schirmeck and later one in the

abgeurteilt und außerdem n
em **Konzentrationslager** üb

Excerpt from a notice posted in Alsace by the Germans showing the word Konzentrationslager, *(concentration camp): " . . . whoever does not abide by this law will be sent to concentration camp after serving their sentence."*

An example question from one of our math books (RM is a Reichmark). "Fritz must buy his Jungvolk (junior unit of the Hitler Youth) uniform. The prices are—shirt: 2.80 RM; pants: 4.85 RM; hat: 1 RM; scarf with ring: 0.75 RM; belt with buckle: 1.75 RM; shoulder strap: 0.85 RM. His uncle gave him 10 RM. How much more does he need to pay for the uniform?"

Vosges, the Natzweiler-Struthof. We knew about them, and stories circulated that the wartime soap was manufactured out of Jewish victims. I never could understand how the Germans, after the war, all denied any knowledge of such institutions. What about Dachau in the suburbs of Munich?

The whole Nazi mechanism, with its well-oiled, grinding cog wheels, was now in place. With Germanic thoroughness, this perfectly efficient meat grinder took control of the smallest details of your life. You had to enlist in the party, otherwise no job, no food ticket, no school. A completely new administration took over, with well-trained officials from Germany. First we were to be shown how to behave, then each person was to be enlisted in various branches of the Nazi party. It was obvious that the Germans didn't really trust us; significantly, no Alsatians could be members of the police.

The names of families deported for "un-German" behavior were listed daily in the newspapers. We knew that the camps existed as we were officially threatened with being sent there.

To attend school you had to be in the Hitler Youth, and that is where my fractured skull came in like providence. Mama obtained a dispensation, and whenever (mostly on Sundays—the party was trying to neutralize the influence of the church) a uniformed Hitler Youth leader came to fetch me, Mama would quickly put me in bed with a wet rag on my face. "Look at him, my poor boy, he's unfit for service." And yet it was with some envy that I watched my school pals in splendid uniforms marching off for fun and sports. These uniforms were all given out for free in Alsace. And what I coveted the most was the Hitler Youth dagger that came with it. This model is still manufactured

I drew this prison car with the inscription on the side: "Schirmeck— Prison Carriage for People's Vermin."

61

Hitler Youth dagger. Engraved on the blade was the motto: Blut und Ehre *(Blood and Honor). "More blood than honor" would have been more appropriate. An excerpt from the advertisement reads: "The dagger is a faithful comrade; your Fuhrer wishes you to have one. Ask your parents to get you one for Christmas."*

today, only the swastika was replaced by the Boy Scout symbol.

Normally, my mother should have joined the *Frauenshaft*, the Nazi party branch for mothers and *Hausfraus*, and my sisters would have been in the BDM (*Bund Deutscher Mädel*), the League of German Girls. But, there again, clever as she was, Mama was able to spare all of us. She asked for an appointment with the *Ortsgruppenleiter*, and in her best High German explained that upper crust people like the Ungerers, the elite of the Reich, had no time wasting their energies with the common rabble, that these people needed an education that she didn't need. *"Heil Hitler, Ja wohl,"* dispensation granted. "What suckers these uniformed goons are," Mama said.

The mail was checked and censored. Every letter mailed abroad was recorded. In the summer of 1942, when I was ten years old, I was sent on vacation to a farmhouse in Regisheim, run by the parents of one of my brother's friends, the Hassenforders, wonderful people who cooked fantastic meals. They had a pig called Hermann Goering. After I got home, I sent them a postcard to thank them for their warmhearted hospitality and wrote: "I cannot wait to visit you again once you have slaughtered Hermann Goering, and to enjoy a good hunk of the Fieldmarshal's ham."

Blessed be the gods in alien heavens! Had this post-card been read by the censors, we and the Hassenforders would have been deported overnight as *Volkschadlinge* (people parasites). In such cases whole families were simply deported en bloc, all their belongings confiscated. The ultimate plan was to rid Alsace of all *Reichland Ungeziefer* (Reich's vermin) and resettle them in eastern territories conquered by the *Wehrmacht*. The constant presence of all these threats, like living under the sword of Damocles, brought the people together. In the shared hatred of the occupiers old grudges were forgotten, and social stratifications were leveled. Now we even had a good rapport with our nextdoor neighbors, the Backs, under the auspices of secrecy and sullen resistance.

According to statistics established after the war, only 3.5 percent of the population of Alsace actively collabo-rated, while across the border in France they were fol-lowing in the steps of Marshall Pétain and Vichy, espe-cially the communists since Ribbentrop had signed a non-aggression pact with Russia.

The new order was enhanced by endless rituals and manifestations, all punctuated by uplifting songs and marches. Who sings together, marches together; and who marches together is fit for the army. In school every week another boy was designated to be *Klassenfuhrer* (head of the class) and responsible for the rituals. He had to come in his uniform for his role as majordomo!

On the hour, as the teacher entered the class, the stu-dents would stand and raise their right arms. The teacher would say, "*Für den Führer ein driefaches Sieg!*" (For the Führer a triple victory!) answered by a chorus of "*Heil!*" three times. Then, "*Ein Lied!*" (A song!) Every class started with a song. The almighty Fuhrer would be staring at us from his picture on the wall. These uplifting songs were brilliantly written and composed, transport-ing us into a state of enthusiastic glee. I still remember

After the war, the Hitler Youth dagger became the Boy Scout dagger simply by replacing the swastika insignia.

The cover of a Diary for German Youth. *It was a special copybook in which we had to write a daily essay about the events on the front.*

them all, and after all these years, if I am tired or depressed, one song and my spirits are restored.

Next came the morning prayer:

Protect, oh God, with your strong hands
Our people, our Fatherland.
And let upon the footsteps of our Fuhrer
Shine your grace and mercy.
Awake anew in our hearts
Our German ancestors' courage and faith
And so let us, strong and pure,
Be your German children.

Then we stepped forward and were inspected by the teacher for clean hands, ears and teeth, for the Fuhrer despised dirty children.

The first hour was dedicated to history—or the rise of the Nazi movement—and the news from the front. We had a special copybook for this. Indoctrination was daily and systematic. Jazz, modern art, and comic strips were considered degenerate and forbidden. I could easily imagine Donald Duck, Mickey Mouse, or Superman and their likes dutifully arrested by the Gestapo to serve in some hard labor squad.

Students from Germany were among us. They were nice enough and they tried desperately to be friendly, but we remained politely distant, and even felt somewhat sorry for them. Actually, school was fun. All subjects were taught in a pleasant way. Everyone did as well as he could, with a minimum of punishment. This was not too difficult since we were told "Do not think, the Fuhrer thinks for you!"

The teaching was very "practical." I had a hard time adjusting to German, but this didn't seem to be too much of a problem. I could draw well, and the teacher assured me in a comforting voice: "The Fuhrer needs artists—he

Great attention was given to the design, illustrations, and photographs in schoolbooks. The use of woodcuts was especially effective as shown here in these two examples.

Ein junges Volk steht auf

Tag der deutschen Revolution

| BDM.-Mädel mit BDM.-Weste und und BDM.-Mütze | BDM.-Mädel mit Mantel | Jungmädel in Sommertracht | Untergauführerin in Sommertracht |

Uniforms of the BDM, Bund Deutscher Mädel, *the League of German Girls. Left, two winter uniforms, followed by the summer uniform of a* Jungmädel, *a kind of "Fuhrer's Brownie" but in a white shirt. At far right is the BDM summer uniform.*

Jungzugführer des DJ.
im allgemeinen
Winterdienstanzug

Jungvolkpimpf
als Trommelbube
im allgemeinen
Sommerdienstanzug

Jungbannführer
im großen
DJ.-Führer-Dienstanzug

Uniforms of the Hitler Youth (Hitler-Jugend). *The boy in the center is wearing the summer uniform of a drummer in the* Jungvolk, *the cub branch of the Hitler Youth.*

Marching drum and bugle corps of the Hitler Youth, Alsace, 1941.

Jungvolk drummers at a rally in Alsace in 1941.

BDM troop at a rally in Alsace in September, 1941.

Alsatian girls dancing in German traditional costumes at a folk festival, May Day, 1941.

Illustrations from an early reader showing (top) a joyous band of singing and marching Jungvolk, *and (bottom)* Jungmädel *collecting money for the* Winterhilfswerk *(see page 126) by selling little synthetic flowers made by concentration camp labor.*

Facing:
The cover of one of my school copybooks.

Hans Ungerer

Ungerer

IV

Klasse   Schuljahr

Heft Nr. 7

Unser Führer

heißt Adolf Hitler. Er

wurde geboren am 20.

April 1889 in Braunau.

Unser Führer ist ein großer

Soldat und ein großer

Arbeiter. Er hat Deutsch-

land aus der Not befreit.

In der hat Arbeit, Brot und

Frieden. Unser Führer liebt

die Kinder und die Tiere.

4

Facing:
The first text learned by heart and written in my copybook in the new script:

"Our Fuhrer is named Adolf Hitler. He was born on the 20th of April 1889 in Braunau. Our Fuhrer is a great soldier and tireless worker. He delivered Germany from misery. Now everyone has work, bread, and joy. Our Fuhrer loves children and animals."

Above, the first page of my first copybook with my teacher's comment on the swastikas—zu klein, (too small). Nothing was too big for the Third Reich.

Die nationalſozialiſtiſche Flagge.

Und ein Symbol iſt dies wahrlich!

Nicht nur, daß durch die einzigen von-uns allen, heißgeliebten Farben, die einſt dem deutſchen Volke ſo viel Ehre errungen hatten, unſere Ehrfurcht vor der Vergangenheit bezeugt wird, ſie war auch die beſte Verkörperung des Wollens der Bewegung. Als nationale Sozialiſten ſehen wir in unſerer Flagge unſer Programm. Im Rot ſehen wir den ſozialen Gedanken der Bewegung, im Weiß den nationaliſtiſchen, im' Hakenkreuz die Miſſion des Kampfes für den Sieg des ariſchen Menſchen und zugleich mit ihm auch den Sieg des Gedankens der ſchaffenden Arbeit, die ſelbſt ewig antiſemitiſch war und antiſemitiſch ſein wird . . .

Adolf Hitler.

A text by Hitler on the swastika from one of my school readers: "In the swastika lies the mission to fight for the victory of the Aryan race, as well as the triumph of the concept of creative labor, which always, in itself, was anti-Semitic, and always will be."

Immediately after the arrival of the Nazis, schoolbooks specially conceived for Alsace were available overnight free of charge.

himself is one." Under the Nazis, painters and sculptors were paid a monthly salary from the state. Difficult for all of us was not only the change of language but the change of handwriting—the German Gothic *Sutterlinschrift*.

I still have all of my copybooks. In the first one you can see my assignment with the swastika flag and the line "Glory to our Fuhrer Adolf Hitler." The swastika was not big enough, the teacher noted. On the next page was the first text we had to learn by heart: "Our Fuhrer is named Adolf Hitler. He was born the 20th of April (my sister Edith's birthday!) 1889 in Braunau. Our Fuhrer is a great soldier and tireless worker. He delivered Germany from misery. Now everyone has work, bread, and joy. Our Fuhrer loves children and animals."

Unsere Schrift

Die Runen

ᚠᚢᚦᚨᚱᚲᚷᚹᚺᚾᛁᛋ ᛃᛖᚺᛏᛒᛗᛚᛜᛟᛞ

Ursprünglich waren sie sichtbare S i n n b i l d e r für unsichtbare, rätselhaft und geheimnisvoll waltende Mächte in der Natur. Der naturverbundene germanische Mensch ritzte sie anfänglich mit dem Messer in Buchenstäbchen, warf diese auf ein Tuch, schüttelte sie durcheinander und las (hob) dann drei Stäbe auf und sprach die Runennamen. Daraus deutete er, ob die Mächte ihm hold oder feind wären. Im Großdeutschen Reich sind einige Runen erneut zu Symbolen geworden:

Die Odal-Rune:	ᛟ	ist das Zeichen des landgebundenen deutschen Bauern.
Die Sieg-Rune:	ᛋ	ist das Zeichen der ᛋᛋ und des DJ.
Die Tyr-Rune:	ᛏ	trägt der höhere SA.-Führer auf dem Ärmel.
Die Mann-Rune:	ᛉ	trägt das deutsche Frauenwerk.

New script: the Sutterlinschrift *was added to the old Latin alphabet, creating a new notched alphabet that we had to learn, as well as Gothic lettering and the meaning of runes. The instructions read: "The Great German Reich has brought back the Runic symbols. Odal Rune: the symbol of the German farmer's attachment to the soil.; Victory Rune: the symbol of the S.S.; Tyr Rune: the sign carried on the sleeve of S.A. leaders; Mann Rune: the sign of the German Women's Corps."*

I devised my own alphabet to write anti-Nazi comments and secret messages. I would seal them in empty bottles that I buried behind the back yard for future discovery in case we were annihilated. Twenty-five years ago I returned to Logelbach in an attempt to dig them up, but a new house stood atop the spot.

Lesebuch
für die Volksschulen
im Elsaß 1940

HOFF-JANN 1940

A photograph illustrating the story of Berta, invited to have breakfast with the Fuhrer in Berchtesgarten on her birthday, "the greatest and happiest moment of her life."

In every cigarette package was a picture vignette, the equivalent of the U.S. baseball card. Here are two of these: Hitler with his favorite dog (an Alsatian!) and with two boys (not Alsatian) in lederhosen.

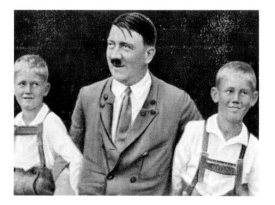

These cigarette vignettes were collected in albums, and made by colorizing black and white photos, which gave the pictures strong contrasts, especially between the red of the flags and the brown shirts of the S.A. The Nazis knew how to feed and exploit the collector's spirits.

Wer leben will/ der kämpft also/ und wer nicht streiten will in dieser Welt des ewigen Ringens/ verdient das Leben nicht+

Adolf Hitler

Every book had an illustration of the Fuhrer with one of his sayings as a frontispiece. Here Hitler says: "Who wants to live has to fight, and whoever refuses to fight in this world of eternal challenge has no right to live."

Our schoolbooks were strewn with pages of sayings from the Fuhrer: "Learn to sacrifice for your fatherland. We shall go onwards. Germany must live. In your race is your strength. You must be true, you must be daring and courageous, and with each other form a great and wonderful comradeship."

Der Führer spricht:

Lerne Opfer bringen für dein Vaterland!

*

Wir sind vergänglich, aber Deutschland muß leben!

*

In deinem Volke liegt deine Kraft.

*

Ihr müßt treu sein, ihr müßt mutig sein, ihr müßt tapfer sein, und ihr müßt untereinander eine einzige große, herrliche Kameradschaft bilden!

Adolf Hitler.

56

The cover and some text from our new German vocabulary manual.

16. The new Great German Reich brought us a new vocabulary. New expressions for the new times: Germany Awake, Common Interest before Self Interest, Blood and Soil, Strength through Joy, Mother and Child, Air Raid Protection Is a Must! Labor Service, Labor Front, Blood Flag, Blood Medal, Hot Pot Sunday, Followers, Equal Rights, Swastika, Hitler Youth, Hitler Youth Cubs, Year of the Soil, Nationalist German Workers Party, Army, Airforce, Winter Charity Work, Chancellor of the People, People's Community, Reichradio, Reich Superhighway, Brownshirt, Region Leader, Administra-tor, Party Cell Guard, Block Guard, Local Chapter, Evening Training, Heirloom, Inherited Farm . . ." We were further instructed to find even more expressions!

We were promised a reward of money if we denounced our parents or our neighbors—what they said or did. I know of no existing case where this happened. We were told: Even if you denounce your parents, and if you should love them, your real father is the Fuhrer, and being his children you will be the chosen ones, the heroes of the future.

In Rufach, the asylum where my shell-shocked Uncle Daniel lived (he mysteriously disappeared during the evacuation) was turned into a NAPOLA *(Nazional Politische Erziehungs Anstalt)* college, a national political institute of education. Alsatian orphans were put there. I have a friend, two years older than me, who was sent to the front, decorated with an iron cross at the age of fifteen and a half, taken prisoner by the Russians at sixteen, escaped after two years behind Russian barbed wire, and, unbeknownst to the Germans, was half Jewish!

16. **Das Großdeutsche Reich bringt neues Sp**
Neue Wörter sind Ausdruck der neuen
wache! / Gemeinnutz geht vo
Boden / Adel der Arbeit / Kra
ter und Kind / Luftschutz tut
Arbeitsdienst, Arbeitsfront, Blutfahne,
folgschaft, Gleichberechtigung, Hakenk
Landjahr, Nationalsozialistische Deutsc
Luftwaffe, Winterhilfswerk, Volkskanzle
sender, Reichsautobahn, Braunhemd, Ga
Blockwart, Ortsgruppe, Schulungsabend,
Suche andere zusammengesetzte Haup
passen!

17. **Die Gegenwart spiegelt sich in den „jü**
wider
Das Geschehen der Gegenwart spricht besonders aus den Wörtern, die
in unserer Zeit geprägt worden sind.
Achsenmächte, Bunker, Flak, Heckenschütze, Krad, Stuka, Versehrter,
rückgeführt, umgeschult, Anlernling, Austauschstoffe, abschirmen, ent-
schandeln, entstädtern, . . .
Gib an, was diese Wörter bedeuten!

Garz - Hartmann - Hänsel - Wiechmann

Arbeitsbuch
für den Unterricht
in der deutschen Sprache
an Volksschulen

ELSASS

Ausgabe L
Heft 2 • 5.-8. Schuljahr

Verlagsgemeinschaft Moritz Diesterweg · Frankfurt a. M.
Alsatia · Kolmar (Elsaß) / Konkordia · Bühl (Baden)

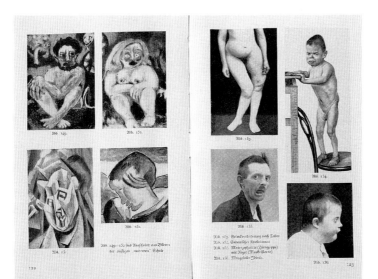

Modern art was considered degenerate. Here, out of a school textbook, is a comparative study between modern paintings and deformed humans. For example, the Modigliani in plate 126 is compared to a person with Down's Syndrome.

Comparing is an Alsatian mania. The French have called us sales boches *(dirty Krauts)*, while the Germans called us Franzosen Kopfe *(Frenchheads)*. We call the Germans schwowe *(Swabian)* and the French hase *(rabbits)*.

Here is a set of cards that I made for playing Old Maid. The pairs compare the French *(loved)* and the Germans *(hated)*. The Old Maid is Hitler.

My grandmother on my father's side had the greatest respect for order and discipline. Before the war she favored the Germans, missing the good old Kaiser times. My drawing of a German soldier says: "For my dear grandmother with thanks, Tomi, 1941." I was thanking her for the toy army truck she had given me for my birthday (pictured below).

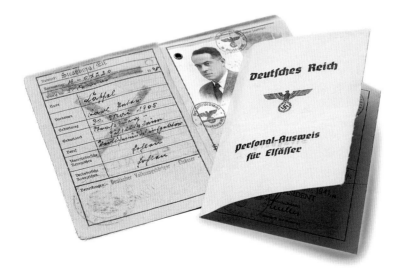

Reint. Stra–VI–9.

B e s c h e i n i g u n g.
=–=–=–=–=–=–=–=–=–=–=–=–=

Hiermit wird bescheinigt, daß Herr-Frau-

Der *Theodor Ungerer* ....geborene.....................

geboren am .*27.7.1894.*.in..Straßburg.*i.E.*..................

wohnhaft in Straßburg .*verstorben in Straßburg am 5.9.1935*

deutscher Volkszugehöriger elsäßischer Abstammung im

Sinne des § 6 der Verordnung über die deutsche Staats-

angehörigkeit im Elsaß vom 24.8.1942 ist.

Straßburg, den .....17.April 1944..........

Der Polizeipräsident

Im Auftrage:

II–m.79–3..4.–

Nr. 4369

Gebühr .....1.–....RM. bezahlt.

Papers and documents were required for everything in life under the Nazis. This certificate (above) was very important—it "proved" that we were of pure "Aryan" descent.

Nazi passport for Alsatians.

Gutachten

über den Schüler Johann Ungerer :

Der Junge scheint etwas zarter Gesundheit zu sein, leidet seit einem Unfall oft an Kopfschmerzen. Die Mutter ist vielleicht etwas zu ängstlich in dieser Beziehung und läßt ihn oft die Schule versäumen.

Johann hat einen guten, hilfsbereiten Charakter, vielleicht etwas zu nachgiebig. Er ist meist still und verträumt, mitunter auch sehr aufgeweckt.

Er ist erst seit Mai 1941 mein Schüler und hat oft gefehlt. Vor Oktober 1940 hat er nie deutsch gelernt, scheint aber gut durchschnittlich begabt zu sein. Besonderes Talent erweist er im Zeichnen.

Logelbach, den 27. August 1941

Die Lehrerin:
Martha Langlaude.

Throughout all this turmoil I managed to have a good time. And while my family taught me French, and the Germans German, I had my new friends who taught me Alsatian, a wonderful, rich language (a friend of mine collected 186 expressions in Alsatian to describe drunkenness). I could go out in the streets and play. I became streetwise.

I kept a secret notebook with a list of the names of all my classmates: the ones who liked me and the ones who didn't. The ones who didn't I worked on and I eventually won them over. My best friends lived in tenements across the street. I had a good friend, Armand, the son of a widow who lived in a small worker's cottage—where there was no nice furniture, or books, or paintings, only proud barren poverty. We led a gang of kids, and how much fun we had! We cruised all over, doing mischief.

EIN
LEHRER
VON
KOLMAR

1947

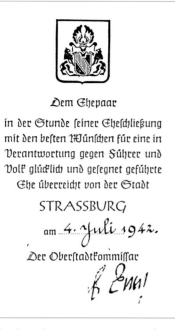

Dem Ehepaar

in der Stunde seiner Eheschließung
mit den besten Wünschen für eine in
Verantwortung gegen Führer und
Volk glücklich und gesegnet geführte
Ehe überreicht von der Stadt

STRASSBURG

am 4. Juli 1942.

Der Oberstadtkommissar

*Newlyweds were given a copy of
Hitler's book* Mein Kampf *with this
special certificate placed inside.*

I still have my schoolbooks. The frontispiece in all of them is a portrait of the Fuhrer, with one of his sayings. The texts are a clever mixture of fairy tale and German heroic deeds, with workers and farmers glorified. Propaganda even found its way into mathematics. History was reversed. It was utterly confusing to be told that Charlemagne was German, not French, and his real name was Karl der Grosse, and that the Franks gave their name to France and by sacking Rome established the Holy Roman Empire (now known as the European Union).

A Dr. Schmitthenner, in a book on art history, went so far as to contend that Leonardo da Vinci was of German origin and that his original name was Leonhard von Wincke. Schiller's *Wilhelm Tell* was not on the curriculum, for this Swiss terrorist might have inspired us Alsatians to follow in his footsteps.

In class I was a dreamer, easily distracted. I was an average if not below-average student, yet I made it to high school, back to the Lycée Bartholdi, renamed Mathias Grunewald Schule.

Excerpts from my school regulations:
The school has the duty to teach its pupils to develop a strong character bodily and spiritually. This is to make them ready for life in upper and leading positions, endowed with political, cultural and economic ability . . .

. . . the only acceptable form of greeting is "Heil Hitler". . .

Every pupil has to contribute to the image of his town, and is not to tread upon public lawns, not to disturb flower beds in public parks, not to cover walls with graffiti, not to drop any type of paper on the sidewalks. These will be punished by the police as well as by the school. It is especially forbidden to torture animals . . . Anyone using insults, obscene words, or exhibiting vulgar behavior will be expelled from school. This applies for every kind of behavior that endangers the comradely spirit and the harmony of the community.

Pupils who are unhygienic, unkempt, or slovenly will be expelled as well.

Every morning I took the bus. There was no gasoline at that time, and the engine ran on compressed gas that was carried in a huge tank on its roof. I shudder to think of the explosion had the tank sprung a leak or run into a wall. The bus terminal was next to the Unterlinden, an ancient cloister converted into a museum, famous for Grunewald's "Isenheim Altarpiece." How many times, instead of waiting outside for the bus, did I go in and contemplate these paintings, which for me (and I am not alone) constitute one of the most important works of art of all time. Grunewald has without a doubt exercised the greatest influence of any painter in my artistic career. I still identify with St. Anthony confronted by temptations. I liked the temptations better than the saint, and it seemed to me absurd that temptations should look so fierce and ugly. My demons would be more like beautifully endowed females and wily cooks with platters of delicacies.

I was from birth a fragile child, plagued every winter with chronic earaches. My constant headaches were encouraged by my mother—it gave her power for me to

My high school report card. It is interesting to note the priority given to sports above other subjects, from which I was exempt, therefore there are no grades. The remarks say: "Irregular performance, misses school too often." The grades went from 1, the best, to 6, the worst. Note that my only 1 came in art.

Matthias Grünewald-Schule Kolmar (Elsaß)
Oberschule für Jungen

Schuljahr 1943 / 44   Klasse: 2A   1. Schuljahrsdrittel

Zeugnis

für Ungerer Hans

I. **Allgemeine Beurteilung** des körperlichen, charakterlichen und geistigen Strebens und Gesamterfolges: Sein charakterliches u. geistiges Streben ist ungleichmässig. Hans müsste die Schule regelmäsiger besuchen.

II. **Leibeserziehung.**

Allgem. körperliche Leistungsfähigkeit: _____

Teilgebiete: Leichtathletik . _____

Turnen			Spielen	
Schwimmen			Boxen	

Die Wertungen in Leibesübungen drücken im Gegensatz zu den Noten in den wissenschaftlichen Fächern den Schwierigkeitsgrad aus, den der Schüler mit seinen Leistungen erreicht hat.

Es bedeuten: 1: den geringsten Schwierigkeitsgrad, 5: die „Normalleistung" der Altersklasse (Mittelleistung) 9: den höchsten Schwierigkeitsgrad.

III. **Wissenschaftliche und künstlerische Leistungen.**

Deutschkunde:

		Fremdsprachen:	
Deutsch	3	Englisch	3
Geschichte	3	Lateinisch	
Erdkunde	2	Griechisch	
Kunsterziehung	1	Französisch	
Musik	2		

Naturwissenschaft - Mathematik:

		Wahlfreie Lehrgegenstände:
Biologie	3	
Chemie		
Physik		
Mathematik	4	

Versäumnisse: 20 Tage

IV. **Bemerkungen:** _____

Kolmar Els., den 31. März 1944

Der Direktor: D. H. Bleicher
Oberstudiendirektor

Der Klassenlehrer: P. Werck
Ungerer

Unterschrift des Vaters oder Fürsorgers:

O. S. 4 - 3513 - K
VORDRUCKVERLAG DECKER KOLMAR

Facing:
A drawing for my
homework about the
"Negro Judeo-
American" Colorado
beetle.

Sammelt Knochen! Sie enthalten wertvolle Rohstoffe

8. Bei Beginn des 2. Vierjahresplanes (1936) verarbeitete die deutsche Industrie jährlich rund 100 000 t Knochen, die aus dem Inland stammten. Durch die Knochensammlung erhielt sie im Jahre 1937 rund 40 000 t mehr. Aus 100 000 t Knochen gewannen die Fabriken 10 000 t Fett (bes. für Seife), 15 000 t Leim und 45 000 t Futter- und Düngemittel.

a) Wieviel von den drei Stoffen konnte man aus den 40 000 t gewinnen?

b) Man schätzt, daß im Deutschen Reich jährlich ungefähr 450 000 t Knochen abfallen. Wieviel Fett könnte diese Menge geben? — Wieviel Leim? — Wieviel Futter- und Düngemittel?

9. Aus dem Fett von 450 000 t Knochen können die Fabriken 475 Mill. St. Einheitsseife zu 75 g herstellen.

a) Wieviel g wiegen die 475 Mill. St. Seife? Wieviel kg? — Wieviel t?

b) Die deutschen Haushalte brauchen jährlich viermal so viel. Wieviel t?

Sammelst du auch regelmäßig Knochen?

Altmetall ist sehr wertvoll

10. 1934 entrümpelte man in Hamburg die Böden und sammelte dabei 9000 dz Eisen und 200 dz andere Metalle.

1936 brachte die SA. im Gau Württemberg-Hohenzollern zusammen: 4670 dz Gußbruch, 2270 dz Stahlschrott, 25 050 dz sonstiges Alteisen und 33 dz andre Metalle. In Berlin sammelte man 1936 rund 100 000 dz Altmetall.

Rechne die gesammelten Mengen in Ladungen von 10-t-Wagen um!

Above:
Homework questions from our math textbook. Two of them read as follows:

Out of 100,000 tons of bones collected in 1939, 10,000 tons of fat (for soap), 15,000 tons of lime and 45,000 tons of fertilizer were extracted.

Out of the fat of 450,000 tons of bones, 475 million bars of soap are produced. What is the weight of each soap bar?

German households require four times this amount every year. How many tons?

Do you collect bones regularly?

In Hamburg in 1934, 9,000 tons of iron and 200 tons of other metals were collected when attics and garrets were cleaned up.

In 1936, the S.A. collected the following in Wurtemberg district: 4,670 tons of cast iron, 2,270 tons of steel, 25,050 tons of iron and 35 tons of other metals. Calculate the number of loads in 10-ton trucks.

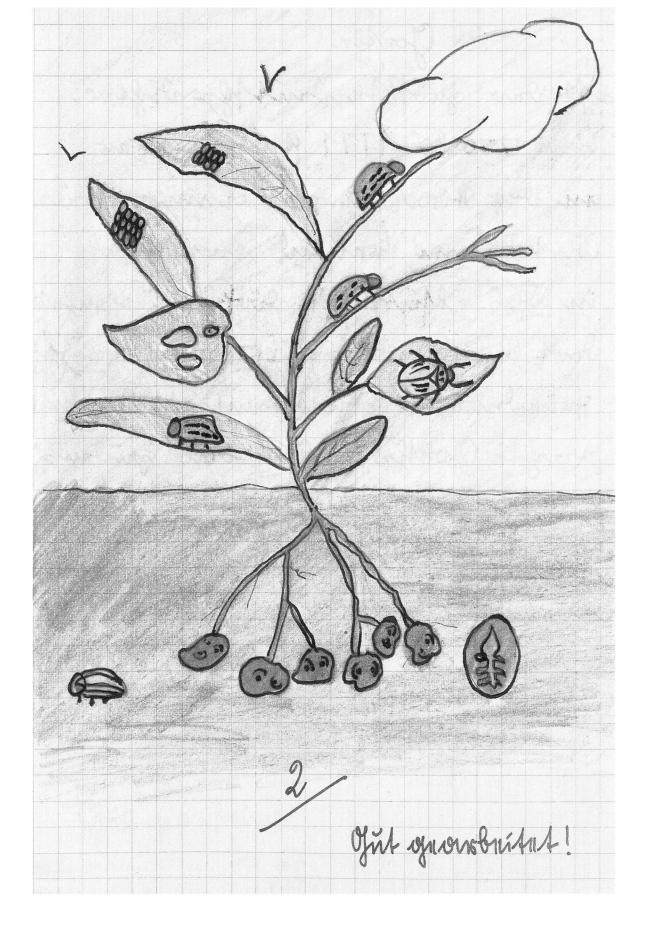

The Vogesenschreck, *"the terror of the Vosges Mountains,"* was a fairy tale Nazi of mythical proportions. Cruising the mountains to catch deserters and black marketeers, he could smell an innocent Munster cheese in a rucksack miles away. I wrote a poem in Alsatian about him in 1943:

Away From Home

I have left my homeland,
My wandering staff in my hand,
Ask me, why have you left?

Because the Krauts arrived.
And when I dream of olden time
When still the French were here,

My heart is sad and heavy,
And I pity all the poor wretches
Who stayed behind.
The Krauts, indeed
They plundered our land,
And the old Vogesenschreck
Sends us to Schirmeck.

In my glossary at the bottom I note that the Vogesenschreck *is a policeman in the Vosges, and Schirmeck is a concentration camp. VLF stands for* Vive la France *and TPLF is* Tout pour la France *(Everything for France).*

D'r Heimatentfarnte

Ir ben doch fort vom Heimetland
D'r Wanderstab in t'hand,
Und wenn mir froid worum ich gange bin ?
So ichs will Schwowe komme sin.

Und wann ich dank an d'alti Zit
Wo noch d'Fransose do kse sin
Do wurd mer's Herz gar trieb und schwar.
Bedire duet ich d'arme Lit
wo noch daheim geblewe sin
Die Schwowe daß esch aller hand
Die han geplundert das ganz land
Und der alte Vogesen schreck (1)
Da scheckt die Lit dert of Schirmeka (2)
Das arme Elsaßland, das arme Elsaßland.

1943

T. Ungy   VLF   T. pLF

(1) Vogese schreck : ... un gendarme dans ce Voge qui arrete tout le monde
(2) Schirmeck : Camp de consentration

Physical education was the top priority in school.

Two postcard illustrations showing the Arbeitsdienst *happily at work. Compulsory at the age of 18, every boy or girl had to serve in these militarily regimented national service labor units.*

be sick. I took advantage of this through my school years and fell sick whenever it suited me. Mama indulged her little nestling with notes of absence from school. My brother frowned upon such practices. I was also rachitic, and ashamed of my rib cage shaped like the prow of a ship. I didn't learn to swim until I was older for fear of my deformity being seen.

I was very happy in high school—new friends, new faces, and teachers who were firm but fair. Most of them were now Alsatians who had returned after their period of reeducation in Germany. We felt that all the Nazi rigamarole was taken with a grain if not a block of salt. Within two years I learned to speak, or rather get by, in English.

It is interesting to look at the school syllabus to see where the priorities lay. First: physical education (I was, alas, excused from it)—athletics, gymnastics, swimming, playing, and boxing were priorities. Then came German, history, geography, art, and music; after that biology, chemistry, physics, and math, and last, foreign languages.

My father in his time played the violin. I was given violin lessons at the music school, but I didn't care much for it and played hooky. One day in town my mother, by sheer accident, met the music teacher. "How is my son progressing?" "Your son, Frau Ungerer, I haven't seen him for months." I was not punished. For Mama it was enough that I had at least some of my father's talents, and she believed you should invest in the talents you had, not in the ones you didn't have.

Each day, students showed up with bags containing everything fit to be recycled—papers, rags, tin cans, bottles, bones, boxes, toothpaste tubes, even horse chestnuts—all part of the war effort. In the winter of 1942 in Alsace they collected 3,963,699 old woolen scarves, and 479,589 pairs of old socks! All of these were stored in the huge attic of our school.

Every Saturday afternoon the whole population had to report to the potato fields, with bottles in their hands, to pick potato bugs (Colorado beetles) that had suddenly appeared, which we were told was part of a "Negro Judeo-American" conspiracy to starve the German people.

The black market became, despite severe punishment, a matter of routine. My mother, with her foxy shrewdness, was an ace at this game. From every Sunday outing in the Vosges we brought back Munster cheese. This was especially risky, since this cheese is known to be the stinkiest among all cheeses.

Our big trumps were cigarettes, because we didn't

My dog, Bouboule.

smoke. They had the biggest value on the market—that is how Mama acquired for me Bouboule, a mongrel dog somewhat like a Hungarian Puli—black and white, hyperactive, and incredibly smart. I built him a cart with a harness to carry my schoolbag. He was a quick learner and played all kinds of tricks, but I was unable to teach him to climb trees or ladders. The only other dog I remember was the milkwoman's German shepherd harnessed under her pushcart, loaded with vats of milk, to help her pull it. Early every morning, she stopped and blew her shrill whistle, and everyone came out with their milk cans to purchase their allocations of milk.

I was absolutely dumbfounded when later in life I found out that German shepherds were called Alsatians in English. And when I tell this to my compatriots, they take it as an insult—German shepherds are still associated with the Gestapo.

There was a gypsy settlement on the outskirts of town with caravans that had windows and shutters and little balconies, and smoke pipes poking out of the roofs. Their homes were fixed in place now that all their horses had been already requisitioned by the French army. The gypsies collected rabbit skins and old papers. They went around with their grinding stones for sharpening knives and scissors, and sold baskets woven from the willows growing along the river. Along with the other peddlers, their cries added to the animation of the streets.

There were no tractors—plowing was done by oxen and horses (big Percherons). Deliveries were made by horse-drawn vehicles. Should a horse drop what were called "horse apples," housewives would pop out of their tenements with dustpans to collect the precious fertilizer. In those days every factory worker was allotted a plot to grow vegetables—a *Schreber* garden, named after an orthopedic doctor who, in 1860, pioneered the idea of playgrounds and garden plots for the underprivileged.

Following pages:
I doubt that anyone or any institution has a complete set of all the postcards from the war portraying the Führer. Here is a tiny selection of this rather monotonous avalanche which, along with prints, busts, and proclamations, systematically engraved the Führer in your memory and dreams forever—all part of a huge, well-orchestrated brainwashing process. The totalitarian regimes of Stalin and Mao used similar methods, but they weren't as successful as Hitler. With his burning passion, Goebbels engineered a propaganda machine unequaled to this day.

Der Führer und Oberste Befehlshaber in Straßburg

Postcard illustration of Hitler striking a heroic pose in front of Strasbourg Cathedral.

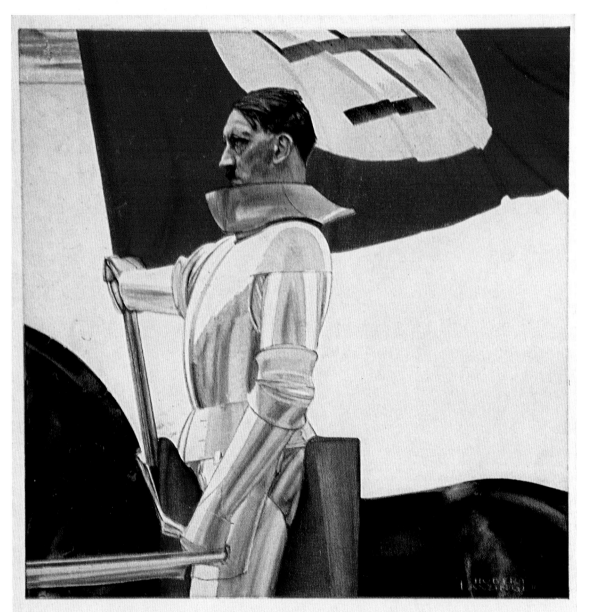

DER BANNERTRÄGER

„Ob im Glück oder im Unglück, ob in der
Freiheit oder im Gefängnis, ich bin meiner
Fahne, die heute des Deutschen Reiches
Staatsflagge ist, treu geblieben."

Adolf Hitler

ADOLF HITLER

REICHSKANZLER ADOLF HITLER

REICHSKANZLER ADOLF HITLER

REICHSKANZLER ADOLF HITLER

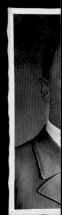

ADOLF HITLER

REICHSKANZLER ADOLF HITLER

ADOLF HITLER

REICHSKANZLER ADOLF HITLER

Reichskanzler ADOLF HITLER

ADOLF HITLER

Reichskanzler ADOLF HITLER

REICHSKANZLER ADOLF HITLER

REICHSKANZLER ADOLF HITLER

REICHSKANZLER ADOLF HITLER

Reichskanzler ADOLF HITLER

Robert Wagner, Administrator of Alsace, a mini-dictator who was given a free hand by Hitler to bring Alsace back, tamed and grateful, into the mothering arms of the Fuhrer. His duty was to crush Alsatian individualism, rid the province of all remaining Gallic influences, and recklessly turn us into a submissive flock driven by "Alsatian" dogs.

He was all wrong—you don't catch flies with vinegar. The Germans were unaware that Alsatians, trained by the adversities of history, were beyond manipulation and coercion.

Wagner's real name was Backfisch, which in German means "a young girl in her problematic years," unbecoming to a Nazi zealot. So he took his mother's name, Wagner. He was a cold-blooded butcher with a forehead much too big for his little brain. After the war he was sentenced to death and executed in Strasbourg on August 14, 1946 in Fort Ney in Fuchs am Buckel (Fox on the Hump) in the suburb of Wantzenan (Bedbug Meadow).

June 21, 1941 remains a date of infamy, when France—under Pétain's Vichy—with servile cowardice officially agreed to the annexation of Alsace to the German Reich. Much damage had already been done, but now it meant that we were fully fledged citizens of Germany. This happened one day before *Barbarossa*, the German code name for the invasion of Russia, which began on the day of the summer solstice. Hitler was keen on the faith of the ancient Teutons and their worship of astrological signs and nature's hidden messages. The Christian religion tamed and controlled with saints and martyrs; this influence was counterbalanced by gods and heroes like Thor, Odin, and Siegfried, who provided fighting, armored warrior spirits. Certainly in Wagnerian pomp you had the choice—after a glorious

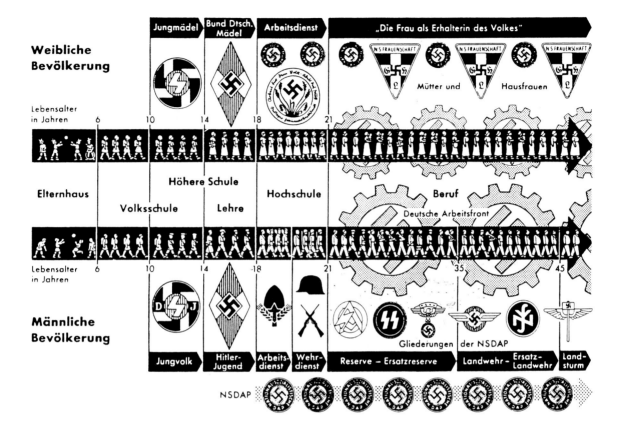

Diagram of the "well-rounded citizen" from birth to death. Curiously, the Nazis didn't think of an after-death organization where the greatest murderers and persecutors would be rewarded with leading positions in hell.

The chart is divided in half, females at the top and males at the bottom. In the center, the various stages of childhood and adulthood are as follows: Ages 0–6, Elterhaus (parent's house); 6–18, the different schools attended, Volksschule (primary school), Hohere Schule (high school), Lehre (apprenticeship). Beruf (adulthood) was spent in the Deutsche Arbeitsfront (German Worker's Union—no strikes!).

For women, from 10–14 was spent in the Jungmädel (Hitler Youth Brownies), followed by the BDM (Hitler Youth for girls) from 14–18; 18–21 in the national labor service, the Arbeitsdienst; and from 21 on as Die Frau als Erhalterin des Volkes (women as safekeepers of the nation). The party branch for adult women was the Frauenschaft.

Men followed a parallel course up to age 18, then spent time in both the national labor service and the military. As adults, they were fully fledged members of the Nazi party.

In this drawing I portrayed one of the daily arrests (I think it was the local baker). The depiction is exaggerated—they didn't have soldiers perform the deed.

It was customary for officers to have their picture taken and printed in postcard size. This one is the living version of one of my caricatures.

death—between Paradise and Valhalla.

Now Alsace along with Baden (across the Rhine) formed one province, the *Oberrhein* (upper Rhine). This meant that under coercion the Germans could draft young Alsatians into the *Arbeitsdienst* (work brigades) and the army (which also meant the S.S., if they were exceptionally physically fit). And so the steamroller was replaced with the meat grinder. Over one hundred and thirty thousand Alsatians were forced into the army to fertilize the Russian steppes. One-fourth did not return. We lost altogether seven times more people per capita than France.

Already, on the 2nd of January, the whole population had been forced to join the Nazi party. Girls and boys aged eighteen had to serve one year in the *Arbeitsdienst*. My sister Vivette was drafted and sent to Germany to do farm work. Many youngsters deserted —at the risk of their families being deported—and many were caught.

Paul, who after the war married my sister Vivette, deserted and was caught at the Swiss border and thrown into prison. Then he was given the choice to redeem himself and save his life by serving with a punitive battalion in Russia—a suicide squad. He came back—death did not want him—and a Russian bullet is still lodged in his leg.

My caricature of a Nazi officer in Alsace.

These times were especially propitious for the acting talents of my beautiful mother. Here is a story that perfectly illustrates the need of such a talent for the purposes of survival. This event was to mark me deeply, and I can say that I remember every gesture, every word with absolute clarity. Speaking French was forbidden by law, but despite the stiff penalties we spoke it at home. As proof, you only need look at my diaries from that time. We were overheard in the garden and denounced to the proper authorities. We Ungerers were not arrested on the spot, but Frau Alice Ungerer was summoned to explain herself. (I cannot clearly state if it was the Gestapo or another of the multiple branches of the Nazi administration.) Mama made herself beautiful, and knowing how the Nazis worshipped motherhood, took me along with her. I was extremely worried, but Mama reassured me by saying something like, Don't be scared, you will see how stupid they are!

So there we were, in a large office decorated with a swastika and a bust of the Fuhrer. My mother raised her arm—so did I. "*Heil Hitler.*" The officer in charge looked somewhat surprised at our spontaneous salute. Pointing to a file on his desk, he said, "This seems to be a perfectly incriminating deposition. It shows that you, Frau Ungerer, who should be an example, insist on speaking French." In a dramatic voice, with crocodile tears in her

Gott Mit Uns *(God with Us)*
on the buckle from my brother's
army belt.

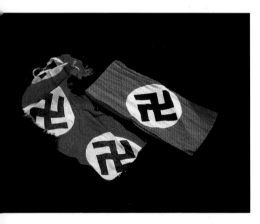

Swastika armbands were handed out
by the Nazis upon their arrival in
Alsace. They hoped that the grateful
population would spontaneously
display them. We didn't.

eyes, my mother replied: "My son, future citizen of the Third Reich, is to be my witness; yes, be witness to the fact that we speak French. This, *Herr Obergruppenführer*, is a matter of education." And winking at me with a sly smile while the officer glanced at his papers, she added, "Yes, we speak French, and you will not stop us from doing so. And I will tell you why. After the war, after our final victory, how shall we establish the new order in Europe, in France, if no German speaks French?" Electrified, the officer stood, came forward and clicked his heels, took a bow and kissed my mother's hand. "I meet, at last, a true daughter of the Fuhrer. Please accept my apologies. Forget these uneducated idiots who waste their time denouncing our elite! Go on, speak French, from this day you will be officially allowed to do so, in the name of our Fuhrer Adolf Hitler. *Sieg Heil!*" "*Sieg Heil!*" my mother answered.

Again and again my mother used her cleverness and cunning. When the time came for my brother Bernard to be drafted, first into the *Arbeitsdienst*, and then the army, she went to the recruiting officer. "Look at these. These are the school reports of my son Bernhard (now with German spelling.) As you can see, he is the best, most intelligent youngster in his class. Are you going to waste this young man on the front, when our Fuhrer needs such brains? He will be able to perform a thousand miracles for the German Reich with his intelligence." She was right—the teachers said he was the best student they ever had. I know because I suffered from it. Starting a new class, the teacher would say: "Are you related to Bernard Ungerer? He was the best pupil I ever had—let's see what you can do!"

So my brother was spared the gray-green uniform. Instead he went on to study law at the university. Only in 1944 was he pulled into the German army, excused from drilling and training by painting patriotic murals on the barrack walls. As an officer commanding a unit of the *Volkssturm* (last-ditch emergency units that enlisted old men and cripples in ill-matched uniforms), he was taken prisoner by the Americans, never having fired a shot. Quickly let out of the prison camp because he was French, he served a stint in the French army.

Some of the Nazis who arrived in Alsace were of Alsatian origin. After World War I, the French had driven out many Alsatians for absurd and unjust reasons. This was the case with a distant uncle of mine, a Protestant clergyman expatriated with his five sons to Germany. One of his sons had now returned, a fascist and a believer, to run the College St. André, now a state school since the Catholic Church had lost all rights to run schools.

German relatives could actually be a blessing in disguise. How many Alsatians, already arrested, were released because of interceding relatives who were members of the Nazi party?

We were invited to their house once, and I played with my cousin Martin, who has remained a close friend to this day. He had a whole set of miniature elastolin soldiers. The French soldiers were just German ones painted another color. We set up our regiments facing each other, and he took one German soldier with a bayonet and knocked down all of my French ones, saying, "You see, we win again. All it takes is one German."

Now we were better off than before—the devaluation of the French franc had reduced our mortgage, the Nazis were handing out allocations for distressed widows, and the Ungerer factory was turning out spare parts for trucks and cars.

One morning the school principal visited our class and announced: *Stalingrad ist gefallen* (Stalingrad has fallen—the Nazis had been driven out), followed by three minutes of silence—for him to wipe away his tears of sad-

An Iron Cross with its original envelope. Ironically, they were manufactured in Strasbourg during the war. This one, unworn, never found a matching hero.

An S.S. insignia pin: a skull and crossed bones. I was very impressed by death heads as a child and this insignia—like a Jolly Roger—tickled my weakness for the macabre.

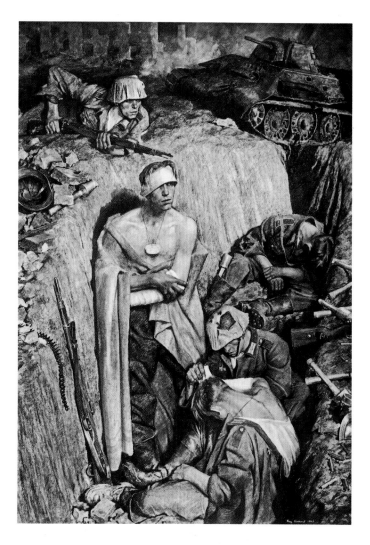

After the fall of Stalingrad when the Nazis were defeated, this postcard was considered to be defeatist and withdrawn from circulation. This dramatic reproduction moved me greatly— in war you don't die, you croak.

ness, and for us our tears of happiness.

Gott Mit Uns (God with us), embossed on every German soldier's buckle, was now our motto as well. At home we gathered in fervent prayers of gratitude, for with this defeat we knew that now was the beginning of the end. The Lord was with us—Mama was convinced that her prayers had taken effect and had played a role in this rout. A free

"...isser ... die **Front** ruft **Euch**

spirit, Mama rarely took us to church. She was not a joiner—the Lord is in our heart, there is no reason to look for him elsewhere. Surrounding her on the piano we sang hymns in French and German. We sang a lot, German folk songs mostly.

A propaganda booklet desperately trying to lure Alsatians to join the German army. "Alsatians, the front is calling you!" Fewer than 500 answered the call voluntarily.

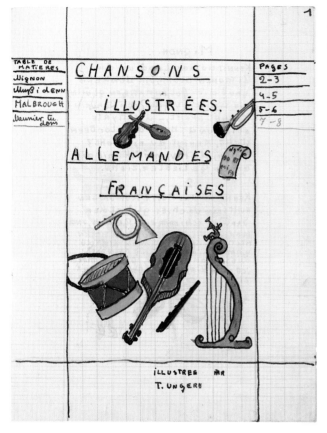

CHANSONS

ILLUSTRÉES.

ALLEMANDES

FRANÇAISES

ILLUSTRÉE PAR

T. UNGERE

Another example of the world I lived in, split by two languages and cultures, is my illustrated songbook in French and German.

Singing has become an important part of my life. With a whole repertoire of songs in German, French, and English I am able to express every kind of mood and deal with any kind of situation, from Edith Piaf (Non, rien de rien, je ne regrette rien) *to Marlene Dietrich; from "Rhinestone Cowboy" to "The St. Louis Blues" . . .*

Yet, when I feel down and discouraged, it is the Nazi marching songs that I learned in school, with their driving force, that get me going again. Even my brother-in-law Paul, who was in a concentration camp, will sometimes join me, sometimes teasingly in front of Germans to whom this is anathema. This shows the deep psychological effect Nazi indoctrination still has to this day on the children of that period.

When I joined the French army I was in charge of training my unit. The French marching songs will not carry you as far as the German ones. So I brought Nazi songs to my regiment, the marching improved, and I still laugh about it. It may seem tasteless, even macabre, but for us Alsatians it is our privilege to ridicule the means of persecution and oppression, thereby exorcising them as well. And our humor, even if black, is not obscured by guilt.

Mignon.

Kennst du das Land, wo die Zitronen blühn, im dunkeln Laub die Goldorangen glühn, ein sanfter Wind vom blauen Himmel weht, — die Myrte still und hoch der Lorbeer steht, kennst du es wohl? dahin, dahin, möch ich mit dir, o mein Geliebter, ziehn.

2

Kennt du das Haus? Auf Säulen ruht sein Dach, es glänzt der Saal, es schimmert Gemach, und Marmorbilder stehn und sehn mich an:— was hat man dir, du armes Kind, getan? Kennst dues wohl? Dahin, Dahin, möcht ich mit dir, o mein Beschützer zieh.

Muß i denn.....

Muß i denn, muß i denn zum Städtele'naus, Städtele'naus und du mein Schatz, bleibst hier? Wenn i komm, wenn i komm, wenn i wiederum komm, wieder um komm kehr i ein mein Schatz, bei dir. Kann i glei net allweil bei dir sein, han i doch mein Freund an dir! Wenn i komm, wenn i komm, wenn i wiederum komm, wieder um komm, kehr i ein, mein Schatz, bei dir.

5

The Nazi song "Es zittern die morschen Knochen" *(The Rotten Bones are Rattling)* with my illustration of the song (facing).

The rotten bones are
    rattling
Of the world on the red front
We overcame the fear
And had a great victory.

Refrain:
We shall keep on marching
If everything falls apart,
For today Germany speaks,
Tomorrow the whole world
    listens.

From the fighting lays in ruins
The whole world on a heap.
What the hell do we care,
We will build it up again.
(Refrain)

If the old ones are scolding,
Let them have fits and scream,
Should all the world resist us,
We shall win in the end.
(Refrain)

They refuse to hear our song,
They think of slavery and war,
And whilst our corn is ripening,
You flag of freedom, fly.
(Refrain)

Nun laßt die Fahnen fliegen

LIEDERBLATT FÜR DIE VOLKSSCHULEN IM ELSASS 1941

Immediately upon their arrival, the Germans handed out collections
of Nazi songs specially printed for Alsace.

The cover of The New Soldiers Songbook.

(inset) The cover of my copy of The Most Beautiful Songs of the Hitler Youth.

These pages and overleaf:
The Winterhilfswerk was an organization that collected funds for indigents, and was originally linked to the Red Cross. At regular intervals, the organization put out objects in miniature that were sold by us kids on the streets. These miniature products were made to be worn on your jacket. There were booklets of propaganda, heroes, songs and fairy tales, as well as hand-colored porcelain figurines, wildflowers, and medicinal herbs. Widely collected at the time, we wondered how such delicately crafted objects fit into the war effort. Later we discovered that they were made by concentration camp inmates. Here are a few examples, many of which are now quite rare.

DAS DEUTSCHE LIED
...CHE LIED
...IEDER
...T 6

DAS DEUTSCHE LIED
LIEDER DER BEWEGUNG
HEFT 2

DAS DEUTSCHE LIED
FEIERLIEDER
HEFT 4

Alte deutsche Volksmärchen Heft 6
DER GESTIEFELTE KATER

ALTE DEUTSCHE VOLKSMÄRCHEN
HEFT 1 BIS 10

Dornröschen
Rotkäppchen
Der Froschkönig
Das tapfere Schneiderlein
Schneewittchen

Der gestiefelte Kater
Hänsel und Gretel
Rumpelstilzchen
Aschenputtel
Der Däumling

WINTERHILFSWERK DES DEUTSCHEN VOLKES

...rchen

...en!«
...ch's
...statt geges- endlich
...mich nun in
...«Die Königstoch-
...r dem kalten Frosch,
...g befahl, daß sie ge-
...e: »Wer dir geholfen hat in

De la plus gentille manière du monde

My talented sister Vivette drew this picture of a fashionable young woman holding a leash tied to a dog with a Nazi cap, swastika leg band, and Nazi flag tied to its tail.

My sister Edith went to the art school in Strasbourg to study costume and fashion design. Highly talented, she was taken under the wing of the *Frau Direktoren*, who gave her assignments designing costumes for the theater and the opera. She was a fervent Nazi, but my sister's inability to learn German didn't faze her as long as Edith eagerly saluted, raising her arm, saying *"Ein Liter"* instead of *"Heil Hitler."*

Bernard had been the head of the family since the age of twelve, when my father died. He was my substitute father, older brother, and friend. We shared the same room, but he spent most of his time studying in the library at my father's desk. My room was chaos, the floor covered with my drawings and multiple activities. It was permeated with the smells of socks and emanations from my chemical experiments, especially mustard gas—the action of hydrochloric acid on sulfates—which smells like rotten eggs. I was a mad amateur mineralogist and performed chemical analyses. I was a hoarder—I later kept parts of a skeleton I had dug up with friends from a mass grave of Black Plague victims from the Middle Ages.

My brother oversaw my homework, and severely checked my school reports. Over my bed hung a sign he had made that said *Sois Tenace* (Be Tenacious), to remind me to finish what I started. He had taken my education into his firm hands, dispensing punishment and rewards. With a great sense of justice and probity, he systemati-

cally instilled in me the basic moral tenets of integrity, honesty, endurance, discipline, and concern for others. I was stamped with these values for life. His own personal standards were set very high, and he practiced what he preached. Highly religious, he was at school a kind of prophet; with his disciples he preached goodwill, passing sometimes as a killjoy when he intervened to prevent mischief. His serious, if not austere, outlook on life didn't keep him from being very funny, and he had a knack for teasing; however, his studies gave him no time to waste. I was lucky, having in him the perfect antidote to my mother's over-indulgence and mollycoddling.

With my mother, brother, and sister Edith: I used the shovel to dig a shelter in our garden. Our family life went on, idyllic, peaceful, just as if nothing was happening. Above left, my two sisters in a romantic pose; above right, my brother teaching me on his last visit home.

1)

2)

3)

Right:

From my school copybook. The teacher failed to notice that in my illustration I was able to sneak in a French sailor with a red pom-pom.

Facing:

The cover of the diary I kept in a now perfectly primitive French. The first page (following) features a complicated secret-door mechanism I had designed to keep my attic room private. (Page 3 of my diary) I was a fervent collector, especially of stamps. It was only in February 1944, as Germany was shrinking, that new stamps suddenly bore the inscription Gross Deutsches Reich *instead of* Deutsches Reich, *as I noted next to this stamp. There is a mention in this diary entry of the platform I had built up in the mulberry tree on which I had built an oven with clay and bricks to heat my concoctions.*

MON JOURNAL!

T. Ungerer (Tête de mort)
1942—44

Cetait tellement vaseux que je nait rien écris.

Lundi le 5 Juillet 1973

Maintenant nous avons les grande vacance. Cette apresmidi je vait cher les Wagner pour Philippe et chez les Walter J'ai aranger mon grenier.

Plan de la mansarde

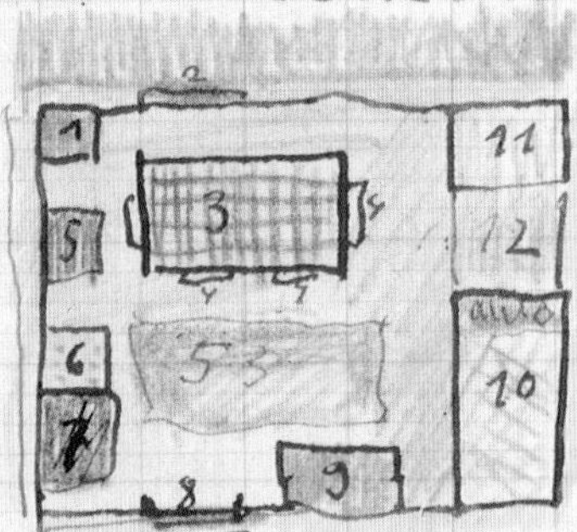

1 et 9 chaises

2 lucarne

3 Table

5 fourneau

6 Table de nuit

7 Cominer 8 porte, 9 armoir

10 lit 12 Tapis etc. couvart d'un d...

11 mall   Porte   5 3 Tapis (viex

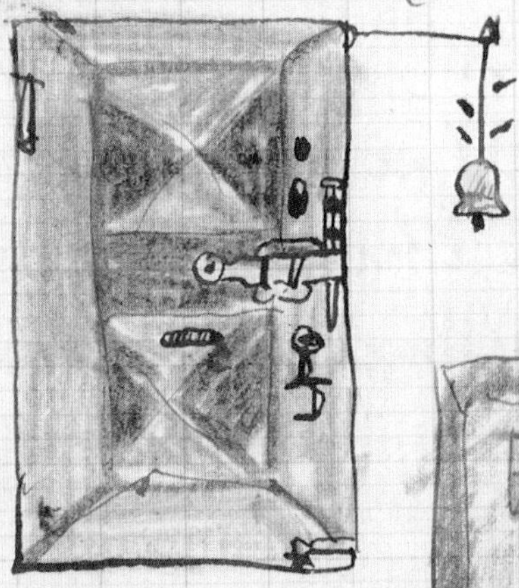

Cloche davertissemen

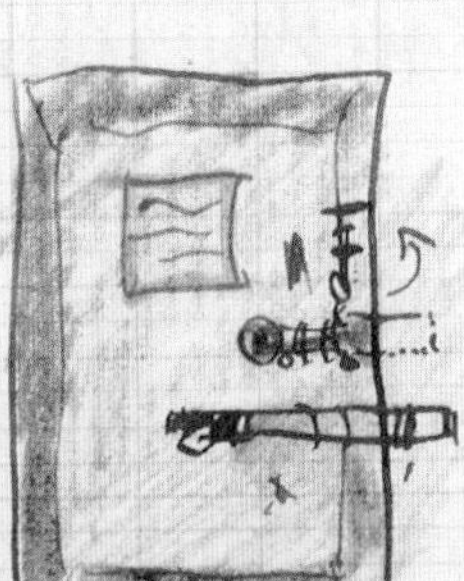

Philipe viendra Jeudi. avec les fillettes
de Mme Wagner je suis aller
at à la foir s'était tres
amusant,

Mardi le 6 juillet 1943
Je suis aller a la foir avec Vivette.
Mecredi 7 juillet 1943
Parti a gebwiler cher tante Susaane
aller a Regisheim chez les Hasenforder
qui me prenne vou les vecanse
la semaine prochaine j'apprent
(quel malheur) Philippe était venu.
Yeudi 8 juillet 1943
Je me lève tôt je prend
l'autobus pour aller ches Philipe
à Kolmar. Philipe etait la; je pare
avec lui ches nous ou nous nous
amuson bien puis il rentre.
Vendredi 9
Je'tait ches Philippe Il etait ches moi
ou s'eit amuser. Bernard viente soir

1847 11 DEZEMBER 1943
ROBERT KOCH 12+38

GROS DEUTSCHES REICH

Robert-Koch-Sondermarke

zu 12+38 Rpf. wird bis zum 15. Januar
1944 anlässlich des 100. Geburtstages
des berühmten deutschen Arztes her-
ausgegeben.
(Presse-Hoffmann, Zander)

reçu

Lundi
J'ai les
Varance de
Noel

Remarque qu'le les
allemand ecrive
Gross deusches Raid
au lieu des Deutsches
Reich tou juste au
moment ou
l'allemagne devient plus
petite

Lundi le 7 Febvier 1944
Les vacance et la faite de noel etait
tres joli j'ai ete tres gater (patin a
roulette avec bague avec tete de mort)
Je deteste les allemand plus que jamais
toute la Ostfront a fichu pour
les allemand je suis mieré que
jamais avec Philipe j'a fait un
fourneau sur la plate forme.
J'ai maintenant de timbre Koch

Stamps stake out history. *From top to bottom: As the Germans marched in, the Hindenburg stamp was imprinted with "Elsass" for local use. Before the war the French were campaigning for couples to have more children. One stamp bears the line* Pour Sauver La Race (To Save the Race). *In contrast look at the German mother blessed with two children, the boy in Hitler Youth uniform. Pétain and Hitler both figured prominently as saviors and heroes.* Marechal Nous Voilá, devant toi, le sauveur de la France! *goes the first line of the Vichy song (Marshal here we come, in front of you, saviors of France). French soldiers, still in trenches, Strasbourg cathedral in the background. Compare these to the martial action–loaded German stamps. In France, stamps for prisoners, women at work and among ruins. German stamps for the day of oath to the Fuhrer, Volkssturm, and model building. The French tricolor glorified the French S.S. units, pictured here like Napoleon's army. These units were trained in Cernay, in Alsace, and were allowed to speak French!*

The quest for food kept us all very busy. I was responsible for the rabbits and chickens. I moved a table and chair into the chicken coop and did my homework there, with the chickens pecking at my slate. I taught the rooster to perch on my shoulder and "cock-a-doodle-doo" in French. I kept a log book of my hens and roosters: name, date of birth, laying quota, date of demise. Every chicken was registered with the authorities (and no doubt they were members of the Great German Fowl Party). After the harvest I would take them out into the fields. They followed me like sheep and gorged themselves on fallen grain.

It was on one of these occasions in August 1944 that a low-flying American P-38 Lightning plane decided to use me for shooting practice. I hit the ground face down and the chickens scattered while bullets strafed the ground. This was when American pilots had orders to shoot anything that moved. That is how, in the middle of the harvest, a family resting under a hay wagon was sent to a better world. The German propaganda had a heyday denouncing the inhuman tactics of the "Negro-Judeo Americans."

In Logelbach, time was told by the chiming of the bells at seven in the morning and evening, and by the factory sirens at eight a.m. and six p.m. These sirens now announced the coming of bomber squadrons on their way to bomb the eternal Reich. We didn't rush to the cellar—we just stood there, watching the shimmering wings of these harbingers of freedom high above us. The smoke of the exploding shells looked like cauliflowers. Long strips of tin foil that were used to jam the German radar screens were gently falling down, sometimes with leaflets. It had an almost festive allure. In school at every alarm we scrambled down the stairs to the cellar where we watched movies. We knew that liberation was on the way.

Facing:
The house in Logelbach, this time drawn by me. In front you see the walnut tree and the chicken coop.

Once, an Alsatian grandmother visiting Germany died in an air raid. Her body was cremated, but as there was a shortage of urns, a tin can like this one for bouillon cubes was used to store her ashes, and mailed home. The accompanying letter announcing her departure to better hunting grounds arrived several weeks later! By then the family, deceived by appearances (if not apparitions), had already brewed the grandmother's remains in a hearty consomme and spooned it off. This is a true story, and when the German edition of this book was published, I received letters about two more such incidents.

The Haussmann factory building that housed the prison camp, drawn by my Aunt Suzanne in 1909.

The prison camp across the street was never vacant. After the French came the Poles; after the Poles came the turncoat Italians who behaved like cheerful gondoliers in *Traviata* uniforms. They were a jolly bunch, considering they were prisoners. And then came the Russians—sick, exhausted, undernourished—sent there because they were no longer fit to work in the salt mines. They maintained the communist order in their camp, and in winter they built a big white pyramid out of the snow topped with a hammer and sickle made of ice. The German prison wardens always had a very lax attitude toward all of their flock.

Our big vegetable garden gave us lots of work to do every day after school, spading and weeding. Watering was especially tricky. The big watering cans had to be lowered into a water hole, crawling with newts. Mama was inspired to go and ask the *Kommandant* of the prison camp for an audience. She explained that she, a poor widow with four children, had not the strength (due to back pains) to tend her garden by herself—could he not then send some prisoners over, volunteers of course, to help? *Kein problem!* (no problem). Every day an elderly sentry was dispatched with a group of prisoners. They all helped—guards and prisoners—and were served a decent meal, and they all returned in the evening with their pockets stuffed with food and medicine and sometimes sacks of potatoes.

In due communist fashion, all was evenly divided with the rest of the sick ward. In gratitude, we were showered with hand-carved toys and objects sculpted by the prisoners. I still have a Russian parrot as a memento.

I went on observing, drawing, taking notes, taking newspaper clippings, collecting stamps and rocks, puttering around, playing with my friends, birdwatching, pressing flowers. At high school I made new friends. My best friend there was Philip Wagner, whose father, a Protestant pastor, had been deported for helping runaways across the border. His mother, with seven children, had been evicted and lived in St. Gilles on an idyllic farm in a little valley at the foot of the Vosges, three miles away.

My wooden parrot, whittled and painted by Russian prisoners. One of many such presents, it still hangs in our kitchen.

SILENCE

L'ENNEMI..

GUETTE VOS CONFIDENCES

French and German intelligence throughout the war was keen on making the population aware of spies. On every wall the Germans stenciled a black shadow with a question mark and the line: Psst! The enemy is listening. For us the enemy was the Nazis, and we really had to watch everything we said (warnings as well as blessings came in disguise). My picture shows a Schupo, *a policeman.*

I did well switching identities: German in school, French at home, and Alsatian with my friends. To survive in this huge spider's web, new standards were applied to morality—cheating, double standards, deception, faking, and lying to the enemy were all considered virtues.

More and more often anti-Nazi pamphlets, of Alsatian (or sometimes German) origin, were circulated.

The big hall of the Herzog factory, further up the street, was used for political mass meetings; huge parades were organized, and along the street, at intervals, huge white wooden columns were erected from which swastika flags were hung. Every household was given a flag that had to be displayed. It was like a carnival except that costumes had been replaced by uniforms. The big celebration days were the 1st of May, the workers' day; the 20th of April, Hitler's birthday; and *Heldengedenktag*, commemorating fallen heroes.

New edicts were proclaimed every day. The tone had changed—the threat was not mere deportation anymore but death. Along with the edicts there was also graffiti: SOS meant Silence or Schirmeck (a concentration camp). Walls were stenciled with a black shadow and the line: Psst! The enemy is listening. Everywhere signs reminded you of the curfew: *Achtung Verdunklung* (Watch out, darkness), and by crossing out the end of the warning you got *Achtung Verdun*.

A *Sondergericht*, a special court of justice, was established to expedite summary executions; thus, a bicycle thief was promptly condemned to death. The smallest joke was severely punished. For instance, in the wake of liberation an Alsatian was overheard saying to a pregnant woman: "You'd better hurry and have your child now, otherwise he will be born French." He was immediately arrested and sent to the camps.

All radios had to be surrendered—owning one was tantamount to spying. We had an old radio that my

I was an avid birdwatcher. These pictures are from my bird book which, like all my other books, was bilingual, as bilingual as my rooster who crowed "kikiriki" in German and "cocorico" in French, and now "cock-a-doodle-doo" in this English edition.

paternal grandmother had given us. She was a difficult case—she loved us children but detested my mother, too beautiful to be Protestant. I had made up the joke that she gave my mother the radio thinking that she would be arrested, put up against a wall, and shot by a firing squad.

Every night we huddled around this radio—Bam Bam Bam Boom, the gong announced the Free French: *Ici Londres, les Francais parlent en Francais* (This is London, the French speaking French). The sounds were hard to perceive—the wavelength was scrambled by the Germans. On a map we followed the Germans pulling out here and there, which in the German news was described as "according to plan." Then came the coded messages: Tonight the suspenders will find their buttons, Albertine's mother has lost her pink slippers, the rabbit will nurse the pig, I repeat . . . This was my first introduction to surrealism.

On Sundays we went hiking with our rucksacks in the Vosges, exchanging goods for food from the farmers. The seasons were marked by their bounties. The attic was scented with all the herbs we had collected, hung up to dry—mint, linden, chamomile, whitethorn, mullein blossoms and others with homeopathic uses. Onions and garlic were also tied to the rafters—there, nature's fragrances seemed to be holding a convention. In the fall we had our fill of grapes during the grape harvest. We collected chestnuts and filled sacks with apples, and brought back buckets full of blackberries, wild strawberries, and raspberries to be put up for preserves. We picked mushrooms, crawling under the low spruce trees to find chanterelles, which would be dried on racks along with apples, pears, and plums.

In the spring we went into the fields to pick dandelions and corn salad. Our walnut tree provided us with

My dream was to become a game warden. Here is my picture of a Tyrolean one.

Mothers were put on a pedestal. This German postcard is typical of many.

Above right:
An egg coupon. Nothing could be formulated simply; words like Reich and Fuhrer crept into every formula. Even here, the eggs become Reich eggs.

cooking oil. In the cellar we stored potatoes and carrots, and preserved eggs in earthenware crocks filled with silicate of potassium. Along the walls of our apartment, on the shelves of a former library, were stored jars of preserves. All summer long it was my full-time job cleaning, boiling, and putting up vegetables and fruit.

It was also my job to fetch food from the attic, and at night I was quite scared going up there using a lamp that I had made by putting a candle in a beer stein, which often blew out, leaving me in total darkness. I was also in charge of starting a fire each morning in the big white porcelain-tiled stove that heated the house.

Evenings were spent around this stove, where we roasted chestnuts and baked apples. The more the situation worsened outside, the more we took refuge inside within our family. We read aloud—poetry, novels, fairy tales. I especially remember Kipling's *Kim* and Scott's *Ivanhoe*. My father's library of books was put to good use. My mother was a gifted storyteller, and fairy tales were her specialty. Many hours did I spend on her knee, listening to stories of evil scheming witches, ogres, and

Die Arbeit ehrt die Frau wie den Mann, das Kind aber adelt die Mutter.

Adolf Hitler

A picture I drew for my mother on Mother's Day.

"Work honors women as well as men. But the child ennobles the mother." —Adolf Hitler.

DAS MUTTERHERZ
ist der schönste und
unverlierbarste Platz
des Sohnes / selbst
wenn er schon graue
Haare trägt / und jeder
hat im ganzen Weltall
nur ein einziges solches.

*Print extolling the German mother.
"The heart of a mother is the most
beautiful and irreplaceable place for
a son."*

perfidious magicians outwitted by radiant fairies, gallant knights, and well-meaning gnomes. I would often do my homework while the others were sewing or knitting. Everyone was always busy.

I spent most of my time reading, and books have remained for the rest of my life my greatest passion. Our house was full of books, and many of them exerted a strong influence on my unraveling education. Most of them would be unknown to the English-speaking reader, but there was also Victor Hugo, Jack London, James Fenimore Cooper, and the fables of La Fontaine illustrated by Gustave Doré. In the huge world atlas I could follow the receding lines of the German front as well as travel with Captain Cook and all the other discoverers whose deeds were consigned to a big volume dedicated to world travelers. My favorite was David Livingstone. In volumes of art history I discovered Dürer, Holbein, the Renaissance masters, and the mysteries of the pyramids.

With children's books I was deeply impressed by the *Struwelpeter* and the *Max and Moritz* stories of Wilhelm Busch that inspired the *Katzenjammer Kids* comic strip in America. Ludwig Richter's *Family Book* filled me with romantic visions. Later in New York I introduced his work to Maurice Sendak, and we both share this influence. The *Petit Larousse*, the French dictionary profusely illustrated with vignettes and plates, especially fed my imagination.

I would lie in bed, staring at the ceiling, and see, as though projected on a screen, Karl May's Indians, the Napoleonic armies of Erckmann-Chatrian, Walter Scott's knights, Jules Verne's Captain Nemo. But I also had nightmarish visions (which I still have) of haunted beings—if I shut my eyes their flattened faces would come nearer and nearer to me as if to ask for help. When I told my mother she took me to a psychiatrist. Rorschach tests only proved that my mental health was not in immediate danger, and that I was simply too sensitive, the victim of an overworked imagination. I was born anxious, scared, sickly—and angry—and simply had to learn to put these drawbacks in forward gear, to feed my voracious muses.

I was indeed overly sensitive. My protective mother was aware of this, and before the war, when Disney's *Snow White and the Seven Dwarfs* was shown at the local cinema, I was not allowed to see it for fear of the wicked queen's effect on my mind. Movies were a rare treat—I remember Spencer Tracy in *Stanley and Livingstone*, and, during the war, *Wenn die Götter Lieben*, about the life of Mozart.

We also had our evenings of real entertainment—charades, solo singing, recitation, and as an ultimate treat, my sister Edith dressed as an Indian princess, shimmying to Rimsky-Korsakov's *Hindu Song* on the gramophone.

In school, life went on. It was fun, and we learned more under minimal pressure. We had special classes building model airplanes (to make of us future pilots in the *Luftwaffe*, of course). One day a fellow student jokingly emptied a jar of model glue on my head—I ran out in a panic to family friends nearby, and in a matter of seconds they poured hot water on my fast-congealing scalp and were able to save my hair. After that incident, the

This illustration published after the war perfectly captures the atmosphere that prevailed listening to the BBC in French from London.

An advertisement for UHU model glue says: "Building models of army and air force planes and vehicles is an important part of your pre-military education. That is why school-children have a special claim to use UHU."

In Alsace we said "Ein Liter" (one liter) instead of "Heil Hitler." It sounds the same. Yet Hitler was a teetotaler and vegetarian. His carnivorousness was channeled into mass graves.

Luftwaffe was out of the question—but I kept my relish for model making.

It was now the fall of 1944. I was twelve years old. We were here, the Germans were here, and the Allies were not very far away and getting closer and closer. As on a weather map, the isobars were infallibly announcing the coming storm. Nearby-based fighter planes—Mustangs, Lightnings, and Thunderbolts—constantly strafing the area were the first messengers of what was to come. This already war-soaked place was to turn into a battlefield again. This idyll in purgatory was about to turn into an inferno in hell. We had to survive our survival. Slyness is of no use with a bomb, and there is never enough time to tell a bullet to get lost.

The Colmar pocket was to remain the last bridgehead the Germans had over the Rhine. Convoys of troops crept towards the Munster Valley to reinforce the troops holding the passes in the Vosges.

A postcard of St. Gilles, my childhood playground. My friend Philip lived there as a political refugee. Situated at the entrance to the Munster Valley, it was turned into a German army camp, their last bridgehead over the Rhine as the Allies surrounded the area.

When German convoys drove by, we children would sometimes cause havoc by pointing our fingers toward the sky as if we saw airplanes, which brought the entire convoy to a halt, with the soldiers scattering to hide in the fields and trucks racing for cover under the trees.

One day my mother and I together decided to take matters into our own hands—we must stop the convoys. In our wagon we loaded all the empty glass bottles we could find, and left after dark on our sabotage mission. We went about two miles to the main road, and there we smashed every bottle. We hid behind some bushes and waited for the next convoy. The moon was shining. As we waited we giggled at the thought of what all this broken glass would inflict on German tires. Instead of the expected convoy, who should appear but a team of workers pedaling home from the night shift. All their tires blew—and never in my life have I heard such a chorus of curses and oaths. Downcast, we went home, shamefaced at the thought of these poor men's terrible inconvenience. During the war rubber products were rare, and tires precious. Sabotage, I learned that night, is better left to experts.

St. Gilles, where my friend Philip lived, became an army camp. And what an army—Sikhs with turbans in

Watch out! Airplanes! With our forefingers
pointing toward the open skies we put
entire convoys into scramble.

Gone were the spic and span units of the German army.
Now vehicles drawn by sad-looking draft horses with bleeding
hooves were carrying supplies to an army of ragamuffins.
This did not apply to some of the elite crack units.

Luftschutz tut not

Herr Müller entrümpelt seinen Dachboden, er füllt eine Kiste mit Sand, er stützt die Kellerdecken, er dichtet die Kellerfenster ab, er hält Äxte und Schaufeln bereit, er stellt Gefäße für Wasser hin, er legt die Gasmasken zurecht, er sorgt für Bänke, er läßt Bettstellen in den Keller bringen, er richtet eine Notbeleuchtung ein, ...

   a) Das muß überall so sein. Alle Dachböden müssen entrümpelt w e r d e n. In jedem Hause müssen ...

   b) Dann kann jeder dem Luftschutzleiter melden: Der Dachboden in meinem Hause i s t entrümpelt w o r d e n. ...

Every day the papers posted the exact time, to the minute, of the blackout. No light whatsoever was to be seen during this time. The slightest ray of light shimmering between curtains was met with immediate reprisal. No streetlights, no car beams—blue-colored bulbs gave the railroad station an eerie atmosphere.

A drawing by Hansi showing a nightwatchman. They were now replaced by a cruising police force. As a child I was scared of the dark. My brother's remedy one night was to wake me up and get me out of bed for a visit to the moonlit cemetery. A perfect cure, and later, how many times, wrapped in a bedsheet, did I go out to scare the lonely passerby? As the war went on I found out that bedsheets were not for the ghosts but for the dead, and, dyed in blue and red, also made a nice French flag.

German uniforms, bearing on their sleeves a patch with the insignia: Free India. Indians, being "Aryans," were justified as being racially correct to fight for the Fuhrer. They had been taken prisoner from the English, and readily changed sides.

The rumbling and grumbling of still distant battles was indeed like the slow approach of a storm. Colmar was being turned into a stronghold, with us on its periphery. Barricades were erected and our main street ended in a wall erected with Jewish tombstones, taken from the cemetry and wedged between rails.

The entire population was moblized to dig trenches and anti-tank ditches. Every day we had to report with picks and shovels. Actually, we had a lot of fun. My mother and sisters had devised a system by which, after toiling whole days, no results were achieved—by shoveling the same loads of dirt back and forth. And again, as usual, my mother figured out a way to be excused from work.

Bernard, in June of 1944, had been drafted into whatever was left of the German army and was stationed not far away. He came home on sick leave with a rash all over his body, wrapped up like a mummy in paper bandages (cotton ones were for casualties on the front). He had already written me a letter explaining that should anything happen to him, I was to be the head of the family. I carried this letter around my neck in a leather pouch like an amulet until he returned. Overnight Bernard was promoted to the rank of officer, and he left on his own path of glory to lay his weapons down at the feet of the first American G.I. he met.

The working pass designated for people digging trenches. Everyone from ages 14 to 60 had to report every day to dig with shovels and picks.

A drawing done especially for school about the Volkssturm *(last-ditch emergency units). Old people were now drafted in the spirit of the anti-Napoleonic rising of 1813. By then, at 14 years old I was already standing by to be drafted.*

The sixteen-year-olds were already gone—I was fourteen and next in line to be drafted into the *"Wehrwolf"* units. A place to hide me from the draft was now more difficult to find. In school we were made familiar with weaponry, mostly the use of the *Panzerfaust*—a handy gadget with a hollow charge that was the tank's terror. In the garden I had dug out a secondary shelter in case our house should be destroyed. The Allies were on our doorstep, surrounding the whole area in a pincer movement. Leaflets were falling from the sky.

My proud upright mother with hat at the side of my not so upright brother in his splendid cadet uniform. His jacket is as shrunken as the German front. This picture was taken on Bernard's last leave home.

With my mother, brother, and sisters, and my dog Bouboule, near the end of the war.

The German soldier before and after.

Anti-Nazi tracts of many types were widespread near the end of the war.
The possession of any such material was punished by immediate arrest, deportation,
and later a death sentence. This picture of Hitler unfolded to form four pigs.

Above: an illustration making fun of the Axis leaders.

Left, below: These small gummed tracts could be stuck anywhere.

5 MINUTEN NACH... 12

DIE SAAT HITLERS IST FURCHTBAR AUFGEGANGEN–
ABER IM EIGENEN LAND !!!

GESTAPO ARBEIT

*Our cellar doors, from a photograph
taken thirty-five years after the war.*

Winter came early with a fierce determination, the coldest we had ever witnessed. The battle was now engaged—the surrounding villages were in flames, changing hands especially in the American sector. If the Germans counterattacked, the Americans would just leave and saturate the area with shelling and bombing.

We moved our valuable belongings to the cellar, as we were now under fire. We entered the cellar through outside doors built into a slope beside the house. There was no gas, no electricity, no water. Light was provided by oil lamps and, later, blocks of suet with wicks. I shared a mattress with Vivette on top of the coal pile. We still spent most of our time upstairs and only ran down when the barrage of exploding shells got too close.

Wreckage is not always the result of war. We had a fine collection of ancient pewter jugs—Mama had decided to clean them, and she left them to dry on top of the old cast-iron stove in the kitchen that we were using now

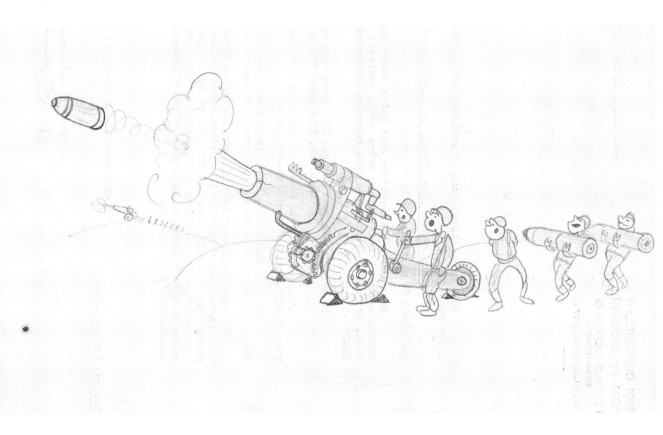

that there was no gas. When she came back to the kitchen she was faced with a pool of molten pewter with a few handles sticking out. We set it all aside for New Year's Eve, to divine our future from the weird shapes that molten pewter formed when poured sizzling into water. It was also customary to read the future in the shapes of apple peels thrown over our heads onto the floor, and to open the windows at midnight to let the New Year in. Not many windows were left in the winter of 1944.

We fetched water from the river (and stuck together for any trips out of the house—if we die, let's die together), but by December there was lots of snow, so for water all we had to do was let it melt in buckets.

I was out on the street when it was hit by a barrage of shells. When the first shell exploded I flattened myself on the ground. Between the salvos, Edith had enough time to pop open the cellar doors, like a jack-in-the-box.

A pewter mug that partially melted on the old kitchen stove that was reactivated when the gas was cut off.

My drawing of the Allied bombing of Logelbach, December 26, 1944.

An Allied leaflet dropped by airplanes inviting German soldiers to surrender.

On the ground, I waved my arms to signal that I was still among the living when Bang! the shelling started again. When it stopped, debris and shrapnel were everywhere, and I ran about collecting it, some of it still burning hot. Further up the street, Herr Berchtold, a stately, fat, mustached neighbor—a good Alsatian—lay in a pool of blood, partially decapitated. He was the first dead person I had ever seen.

On November 23, 1944 we heard on the radio that Strasbourg had been liberated by a daring operation of the French Second Armored Division of General Le Clerc.

We were wedged between Americans moving in from the north and French troops coming from the south—and shelling from both sides. We still spent most of our time upstairs. We were all sleeping in my bedroom where we had barricaded the windows with mattresses. Sometimes at night, wrapped in blankets and giggling hysterically, we would move to the cellar, a risky expedition because we had to go outside. It was very cold, and I wore newspapers under my sweater.

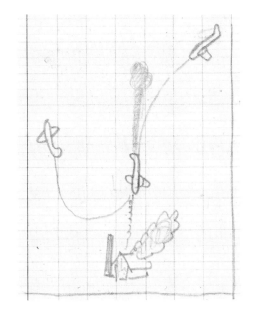

My diagram of a dive-bomber.

My letter to Bernard in the Wehrmacht:

Dear Bibi,
Eight days already under whistling 75-caliber shelling. There is not a moment of peace. Some shells exploded 50 yards from the house. Our street is not a street anymore. The tiles have flown off the roofs, walls are pockmarked by shrapnel, the trees are shredded, the place is covered in bomb craters. The street is strewn with collapsed walls, the meadows flooded, the canal gone. We are intact. No gas, no electricity, no water. The battles illuminate the night. Have no fear, the front is a few miles away. I hold you in my arms with love. Your brother

Christmas was approaching. As a substitute for the traditional tree I went out and cut branches from a spruce tree and piled them up on the corner cupboard, which worked out fine once it was decorated with the traditional ornaments.

On the afternoon of December 26 we were all sitting around the dining room table when the sky outside was suddenly illuminated with red flares. The drone of approaching planes could be heard, Thunderbolts ready for a party of dive-bombing. Nestled in the factory across the street were German batteries, and the flares had been dropped to signal their location. On our floor was a dark walk-in closet, where we ran as the first bomb exploded, clinging to each other and howling. Our four bodies formed one mass; between the roar of the diving planes and the bombs hitting were a few vacant seconds of silence—will it hit us, or not? Each explosion literally shook us, throwing us against the wall.

Then it suddenly stopped, and we stepped out of the closet. What a mess, but a lucky mess—we had not been directly hit. Windows were blown to smithereens, the

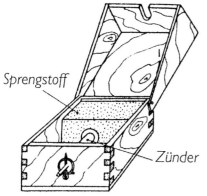

Sprengstoff

Zünder

The battle is raging. This picture drawn afterwards is pretty accurate considering the outline of the Sherman tanks and the American M.30 machine gun.

One of the greatest tragedies was the land mines. Cleverly the Germans used mines made of wood and glass that did not react to the mine detectors. The wooden ones are now rotten, and the cases for the glass ones (above) are still in use as ashtrays in Alsatian living rooms.

curtains hung in shreds, and everything was covered with bits of plaster from the ceiling. The only sound was the crackling of fire—the factory across the street was in flames. We started to perform a little dance, stamping out the sparks that flew in like fireflies through the windows. The roof had lost most of its tiles. On the kitchen table, like a huge present, lay a beam that had flown through the window from a building across the street. They say a broken mirror brings bad luck—the large mirror in my mother's bedroom had been ripped from the wall and was lying face down, unbroken.

In the front yard just by the steps was another providential present from the sheltering sky, quietly waiting for us—a 200-kg bomb, black with two yellow stripes, like a tamed wasp. This dud had hit the ground at an angle, curved, and popped out only to lie down on its belly. It remained there for a month and a half like a faithful watchdog. Had it exploded, the whole front of the house would have gone to meet the fate of all the neighboring walls. The only victims that day were my friend René's rabbits running down the street like little balls of fire.

The German prison guards and their Russian prisoners were helping to put out the fires and help people move their belongings out of the burning buildings. It was close to zero degrees and there was no water to drown the fires.

I don't remember any of us being especially upset. The fact that the Allies were so near filled us with another fire—of hope and joyful expectation. My sisters, using old sheets and dye, had already sewn a big French tri-color flag. The red turned out more burgundy than vermillion, but it was a nice flag all the same, fit for displaying.

Now we only lived in the cellar. Our neighbors the nuns moved in with us. A latticed partition separated our two communities. For Mama it was an ordeal to be forced into such close contact with these papists. She actually believed that Catholics didn't go to paradise, and that the Pope was the Antichrist. To counter the droning of their monotonous litanies, we would intone in firm strong voices Protestant hymns that could only be silenced by the explosions outside. But God would have needed a hearing aid to hear my mother's supplications in this din!

It was a most romantic set-up. Imagine these sisters in their black robes and starched cornets, huddled around a candle, protected from drafts by open umbrellas. One of these nuns had a serious urinary problem. She sat most of the time on a white enamel bucket. The nuns were soon evacuated to better bunker facilities, and were almost replaced by another apparition.

One night the cellar doors were lifted and there stood a young German officer, haggard, covered with snow, and caked with mud. He sized up the place and

A postcard showing Allied troops spanking their German counterparts.

155

said, "Everybody out, get your things and move to the official bunker across the street." My mother, composed, got up and said, "My poor young man, what is happening to you?" He was looking for a shelter to accommodate his truckload of wounded soldiers. "Please sit down. You look like my son who is in the army too, God knows where. There, you are frozen. Have a glass of schnapps, and keep the bottle for your men. Look at this place, it's

With René Ohl in 1992, holding the French flag that was stitched into his mattress.

perfectly unfit for your wounded men; it's cluttered, much too small . . ." The officer left, thanking my mother profusely for her kindness, to look for another shelter to house his pitiful leftovers. In the factory there were still bunkers from the First World War, now used as an ammunition depot. It had its own electric generator on the canal, and that is where most of the population took refuge.

My best friend at this time was René Ohl, two years younger than me. We later joined the Boy Scouts together and have remained in touch ever since. René lived in a small tenement across the street (it was his twenty-eight rabbits that were burned during the bombing).

René's grandfather, a small, wry character with a big mustache, was a veteran of the French Foreign Legion and an unflinching patriot. He was loudmouthed and didn't chew his words, he spat them. It was a miracle the Nazis never arrested him. One night before one of the great Nazi parades, the white column with the Nazi flags had been toppled over. There was an investigation, but in vain, and René's grandfather, one of the culprits, was never caught (his own French flag was stuffed inside René's mattress). You must understand the solidarity—instilled by the Popular

Front—that existed among workers at that time. Alas, René's grandfather died two days before the liberation. In the cemetery a hole was hacked out of the frozen ground. There was quite a cortege, slipping on the ice, ducking and crashing under the shell fire. As there were no coffins, a long and narrow army locker was used that was longer than René's grandfather, and with every explosion his body slid and you could hear the hollow sound of his head bumping against the end of the locker. At the cemetery the grave turned out to be too short. The rotund priest recited his blessings while someone fetched a saw to shorten the improvised coffin. Just like a magician's trick the box was shortened but not its contents.

The 2nd of February was a clear day: there were no clouds in the sky, only veils of smoke hovering over the burning ruins. The snow was melting and being replaced with mud. And the stillness—you could have heard a bomb landing in a haystack. There was something indefinable in the air. The outlines of objects were so sharp in the light that there was no depth to them. The Vosges, trees on the plain, and our garden wall fell away, flattened as on a screen. My sisters and I climbed up to the attic to look out—across the fields, the black specks zigzagging in the distance were tanks and armored vehicles advancing in our direction.

A postcard depicting De Gaulle with Marianne, the symbol of France, as his bride.

"*Ils arrivent!*" (They are coming!) We ran down the stairs, down the street, across the fields to greet our liberators. The Germans, dug into their positions, with crossed arms, smilingly let us pass. One even remarked, "It's all over now."

We ran, and we were not alone. The Russian

Scenes of the liberation. Hansi, back from exile, drew this postcard in honor of the liberation. Old fashioned as he was, he didn't realize that uniforms had changed, and it is still an old poilu *in a WWI uniform who salutes the Alsatian girl bearing peace laurels. Was he too chauvinistic to accept the idea of Free French troops wearing American uniforms?*

An illustration of Churchill bombarding the Germans with cigars.

A postcard illustration depicting an African American G.I. kicking a German soldier out of France.

The banner reads: "Welcome, Long live the Allies, Thanks for deliverance."

Sketch of a French soldier butting a helpless German soldier from behind.

prisoners, who were let loose, and everyone else ran as the news spread like itching powder. It was sheer folly—at any time the place could have turned into a battlefield (not to mention the mines). We welcomed the tanks. The first one was a Sherman; it stopped, the top opened, and for the first time we heard a French voice—an officer with the French First Army. He gave us some Camel cigarettes and said, "See you later, we have to keep rolling!"

What a moment. We went back to our house—or what was left of it. It was like on being on stage walking from one act to another. In a pincer movement the Americans had moved from the other side; they held us at gun point while searching the buildings for German snipers and plundering our home for food and souvenirs. They walked away with our last two pots of jam, which we had kept to celebrate the day of freedom, as well as a few objets d'art.

The Americans drove off in their jeeps with bric-a-brac. This was nothing compared to the later convoys of French trucks loaded with German furniture driven across the Rhine. Who was stealing from whom, and why?

The Russians were well informed: within twenty-four hours communist commissars showed up and whisked their imprisoned comrades to another "paradise." There were other Russians too, mostly White Russians and Ukrainians who had joined the *Wehrmacht*, a motley, underfed band of ruffians who fought in the area and at one point were stationed in the factory across from the barbed-wire-enclosed prison camp. René Ohl told me how he witnessed an argument followed by a fight, after which one soldier was simply strung up in a tree. They had, I am sure, their own sense of justice. The unit left, leaving the body dangling in view of the Russian prisoners—Mother Russia has many wombs! Anyway, they were all executed after the war.

Again a change of prisoners—this time they were Germans. They had suffered fourteen thousand dead defending Colmar, and twenty-three thousand prisoners were taken. Their uniforms in shredded rags, exhausted, with caved-in expressions, they stood waiting in line to register for POW status. They were mishandled, and I watched how, for no reason, some French soldiers were hitting them randomly with the butts of their guns. This disturbing vision canceled out whatever hope and innocence I had left. I hadn't expected the French to behave that way.

At home, *c'etait la fête*, it was a celebration. The French were quartered with us again, another breed altogether (unlike those of 1939), a communications unit of young *pieds noirs* (French from North Africa). Their half-track truck was full of radio equipment. The head of this unit, a liaison officer, took me along in his jeep as a translator, since I could speak English. I helped him communicate with the Americans. I was able to travel around the area, where I saw entire villages that had been wiped out. In Siegolsheim I saw an old woman step on a mine and land on bloody stumps.

We were disenchanted with the Americans. They seemed to behave like well-fed babies, chewing gum, and didn't seem to care whether they were in France or Germany. Our celebrations and enthusiasm left them cold. In my eyes they didn't act like soldiers—they didn't seem to care very much for their equipment, and I never saw them drill. They would throw chewing gum and chocolates on the ground and watch us scramble to get a morsel. To me they were like amateurs. They weren't really arrogant, just aloof. To them we were part of a

Fierce battles raged in the wine district. The cellars were used for shelter and for drinking. Here is an American G.I. in full battle gear.

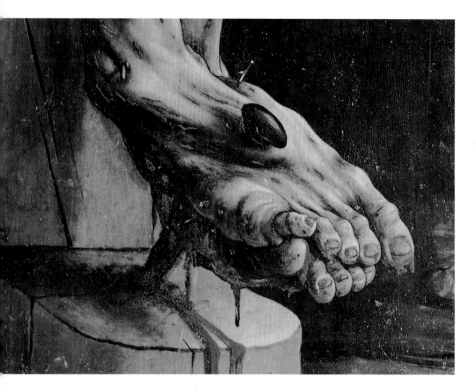

A detail from the "Isenheim Altarpiece," Grunewald's masterpiece (painted c. 1512–1515).

(Below) I did this watercolor three years after the war. The war and the Nazis have influenced my work to this day.

"zoo of savages." But impressions do not make history—the Americans fought and many died on our soil, for which we are eternally grateful.

This was the time of one great festival, with a party every night. The radio and the gramophone provided endless music for dancing. We cooked together with the French soldiers, and I was introduced to the canned gastronomy of baked beans, Spam, and corned beef. The K rations were miniature cornucopias. One ration contained a chocolate bar, chewing gum, cigarettes, toilet paper, vitamin cookies, canned goods, sugar, coffee or tea, and a portable can opener, and—unlike in the German army—no condoms.

With the Germans gone, we became fully aware of the horrors of the concentration camps. Twenty miles from Strasbourg, the Natzweiler-Struthof camp had been built in an idyllic setting in the Vosges mountains, commanding a beautiful view of the valley. There in front of scaffolding used for hangings, prisoners were welcomed by Kommandant Kramer. They came in convoys called *Nacht und Nebel* (Night and Fog). They were made to perform hard labor in the granite quarries. The gas chamber was called the *Abstelltraum* (switch-off closet). The winters at this altitude were unbearable for men in *sabots* (wooden shoes) and no socks. But it was also unbearably hot in the building housing the crematorium that, as it was told, was sometimes red from overheating. *Herr Doktor* Hirt, at the Anatomical Institute in Strasbourg, was supplied with plenty of bodies—live and dead—on which to perform his research.

The camp is still there and is now a national monument. Several years ago the museum in this memorial was set on fire by a neo-fascist gang. I go there on pilgrimage about once a year. I've taken my children there. Along with Grunewald's "Isenheim Altarpiece," this is a sight that has marked me for life.

The gallows (above) and oven in the crematorium at the Natzweiler-Struthof concentration camp.

A piece of barbed wire from Natzweiler-Struthof serves as a constant reminder.

Animated pull toy—the Allied soldier kicks the German soldier. Made in Alsace.

The Germans are driven out. Neuf Brisach is a border town on the Rhine.

I had turned my room into an arsenal: one light machine gun MG.42, one *Schmeisser* MP.40 (a paratrooper's folding machine gun), spaghetti powder used in shells, and cases of German hand grenades called "rat tails." Once, my friends and I dug a hole and filled it with a cocktail: at the bottom was a hand grenade—you unscrewed the cap, inside of which was a string that, if pulled, activated the detonator; you simply tied another string to it and pulled it from a safe distance. On top of that we filled the hole with spaghetti powder and a canister of gasoline—a forerunner of napalm. On top we rolled a big rock, pulled the string, and off it went. The stone went up zigzagging in the air and landed through the roof, which was half gone anyway.

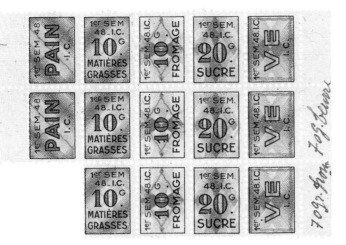

How much more colorful were the French ration coupons, printed in colors giving our stomachs a rainbow.

Jean Boutry, my future brother-in-law, in front of his Mustang.

Day in, night out, the liberation was a huge festival. Here is my sister Edith riding a French soldier on the ultimate cavalry charge to victory.

Facing:
This poster was drawn by Hansi as
an antidote to its German equivalent
(see page 63), and how fine it turned
out to be. The French cultural tank,
with centralized Parisian arrogance,
moved in to crush and wipe out our
identity. The tank is now gone, times
have changed, but the harm done
cannot be undone.

Otherwise we went to the gravel pits on shooting binges. Accidents occurred later when, out of ammunition, we started to make powder with coal, saltpeter, and sulphur. We avoided nitroglycerine, easy to manufacture but extremely dodgy to handle.

Jean Boutry, a young pilot who flew Mustangs in the Normande Nieman squadron, was a frequent visitor and soon started courting my sister Edith. He had a talent for cooking, and through him we discovered a whole new world. I had never tasted a grapefruit or a pineapple. I was unaware of all the different kinds of French cheeses. I nearly passed out when I ate my first couscous—I knew nothing of hot peppers. Every visit brought new surprises. Jean was my hero and I developed a keen interest in airplanes. One day he flew just a few feet over the house and terrified the whole neighborhood. Despite the armistice we thought the Germans were coming back to strafe us.

Bernard was back, as well as Paul, who was later to marry Vivette. After Paul's odyssey on the Russian Front and in Nazi incarceration, it was his mother (my mother's best friend) who, ironically, was killed by shrapnel in the Colmar pocket.

At the time of the liberation the Reichmark was quickly devalued, thus shrinking, yet again, my mother's debts, turning us unwittingly into war profiteers.

The Marshall Plan was now in full swing, but the French made an error in ordering their food supplies: instead of wheat, they ordered corn, because *blé*, the French word for wheat, was translated into corn (which

Children playing with a machine gun abandoned by the German army.

"It's chic to speak French." This sign announced a new kind of tyranny; we were now punished for one word of Alsatian. Liberté, Egalité, Fraternité *is what we yearned for. I found out then and there that we are not born equal, we only die equal.*

This drawing made after the war depicted my anger and state of disarray.

is what the English call wheat). So shiploads of cornmeal arrived, and our bakers had no idea how to use it; they baked baguettes, but inside the golden crust was an unrisen yellow paste.

In the fall it was back to school, re-renamed Lycée Bartholdi. We were given new blue copybooks—a present from Canada. The janitor would come every day to fill the ink pots on the desks and distribute vitamin cookies. I was to be quickly disillusioned seeing the French making the same mistakes as the Nazis—the entire beautiful school library was emptied and burned in the yard, along with films and everything of German origin. Goethe and Schiller went the same way as Heine and Thomas Mann. Even the plaster busts of Greek and Roman philosophers were smashed. The library was a big room with columns, baroque murals, and gilded stucco ornaments. I visited it with a television crew in 1982, and found it the way it had been left in 1945, vandalized by patriotism, shelves empty, and books scattered on the floor. (Irony of ironies: while I was there I tripped over a book written by my grandfather! Another book had a library card with my name—Hans Ungerer.) Happily, the library is now being restored to its former grandeur.

The changes in school were traumatic for me and my friends. It was forbidden to speak Alsatian or German, and we were punished for every word uttered. Everywhere signs proclaiming *C'est chic de parler Francais* (It's chic to speak French) had replaced portraits of the Fuhrer. We had a crop of new teachers, some of them French, and others were Alsatians who had chosen to stay in France during the war. For some we were nothing but scum, a brood of collaborators. Alsatian would still be forbidden twenty-five years after the war—a deep blow to our identity. Alsatian is a German dialect. With our heavy accents we passed for *sales boches*, dirty Krauts—deeply insulting to us, who did not carry the

Germans in our hearts. We had suffered as much, if not more than the others. Again we were branded.

I plunged into French literature with enthusiasm. I could afford the cheap yellow Garnier classics of the old French authors who were not on the curriculum. My fervor was quickly chilled by the remark my sneering teacher made: "Lose your accent before you get interested in literature." Well, I never lost my accent *or* my love for literature.

We Alsatian students had already lost a year in 1940, and now most of us were to lose another year. The French kids, although younger, looked at us with contempt—to them we were German hicks. We kept our distance. This was to change in a few years.

The whole texture of our society had to be mended again. The Germans were gone, the French had returned, as well as the Alsatians who had been evacuated to France and had chosen to stay there in 1940, whose belongings had been confiscated (who were known as *baute Deutschen*—booty Germans—and by the Alsatian term, *Hergelofeni*). It was hardest for the Jews—their numbers decimated, they had come back to a total vacuum. The French (and many others) felt estranged. There was a climate of distrust, and yet in all of this it seemed that we were the patriots, more French than the French, putting De Gaulle on a pedestal.

Back from the war.

The Alsatians caught and imprisoned by the Russians now began returning through Iran and the Near East. Families waited at the station anxiously holding photographs of their sons lost in action, looking for their loved ones among the hordes of returnees.

German school and university diplomas were worthless, and grown-up survivors of the war had to go back to school. We were in awe of their ravaged faces. They hardly ever spoke. One day, one of these veterans was called to the blackboard to recite Victor Hugo's *Waterloo*

The ex-soldier student teaches the teacher. "War has no beauty and no heroes."

Years later I was still obsessed with drawing "the war."

(every day we were given texts or poems to learn by heart). He performed miserably, tripping over the lines and mumbling his way through, until the teacher interrupted him: "What's wrong with you? Can't you feel the martial beauty of this poem?" The veteran grabbed the teacher by his jacket and said, "Don't tell us anything about the beauty of war literature—I've come back from Russia and, believe me, war has no beauty and no heroes."

Our French teacher was a born sadist, a big fat pink toad who wore dark glasses. A necrophiliac, in a trance-like state he would rant on about the beauty of cadavers. When Alsatian students were called up to recite he would grab one of our ears; the moment we stopped reciting he twisted the ear until we were on our knees. The French boys were automatically good students and were not subject to this treatment.

I lived in dread of this man. One day, when I hadn't finished my homework, I wrapped my right forefinger—the same one used to stop the German convoys—in a bandage, and told the teacher that I had cut my finger and was not able to write. He was no fool; with a smug expression he said: "Ungérerre. Rip off this bandage." So I did—in utter shame. With my Protestant upbringing I can say that I had never lied or cheated before in my life, and now, for one mistake, my reputation was gone—and my pride. This was noted in my school record: "This pupil is a liar." To me this was a life sentence, later to be enhanced by the school director's remark: "Perverse and subversive," a sagacious observation since these were the exact qualities needed to deal with crooked situations in twisted times. His remark may have been because of my efforts organizing strikes for the right to speak Alsatian. So I was put on a blacklist, my very own; when I ripped off my bandage I ripped away my childhood.

How many teachers have turned into executioners? My class of 1945–46.

And yet I had some wonderful teachers. The bad ones can traumatize you, but the good ones open windows in barren walls. There were teachers who stood by me and defended me, otherwise I would have been thrown out of school many times. Monsieur Barthel, my chemistry teacher, obtained special permission for me to stay after school and serve my punishment hour classifying and sorting the collection of minerals still bearing German labels. Some had no labels and I could use the school's lab to analyze and identify them.

Later on our math teacher, Madame Perot, flew in like an angel. She embodied what we expected of France. Her French was enunciated in the most beautiful way. She was very thin and sharp, eyes sparkling behind steel-rimmed glasses, and I could never figure out how such a big heart could fit in such a small rib cage. Her love of literature and humanity was without borders. With her we soared. She was a muse to me. She taught mathematics as a basis for rational thinking: how geometric laws applied to poetry, how every book had to be conceived sytematically with all the entailing trigonometry, and that even surrealism was structured by the absurd. She gave me a leather-bound book of blank pages for my poems. We were free to visit her after school for tea, when we would talk, mostly about literature and history.

I was greatly influenced by Sartre and Camus, and became an existentialist. After the war this was the fashionable philosophy. I still identify with Dr. Rieux in *The Plague* and, accordingly, I devised my own motto in life: Don't hope, cope.

The French school system was very severe—a whole scale of punishments kept us muted and crushed. I later quit high school after failing the baccalaureate (the examination required to graduate).

I wilted in school but away from it I bloomed with my hobbies, my books, and most of all the Boy Scouts.

Facing:
"Out with the Kraut trash."

One of my Weltschmerz *faces drawn after the war, influenced deeply by the poetry of Rimbaud, Verlaine, and Jacques Prévert.* Weltschmerz *translates as sorrow mixed with pessimism.*

It was the Germans who gave the new Boy Scout a taste for uniforms.

To be one was my dream. My brother was one before the war; his uniform fit me now, with the broad-brimmed hat, similar to the ones worn by U.S. troops during World War I. Right after the liberation of Alsace the papers announced that a first Boy Scout meeting would take place. At last, it was my turn to wear a uniform. I went, wearing my brother's old outfit covered with badges, my walking staff in hand. When I showed up, they looked at me as if I were a juvenile ghost. They couldn't believe it. I felt arrested and put on trial in front of this grownup, if not elderly, committee of old-timers. "Where did you get this uniform? You have no right to wear it!" I was chided, reprimanded, told I had no right to disguise myself. If I wanted to join I should put down my name and address and I would be contacted. The budding Boy Scout went home and eventually became one.

After the war we traveled to Normandy to celebrate Edith's wedding to Jean, her air force pilot. Vivette was maid of honor, beaming in a dress sewn from bedroom curtains. There, as I began sorting out my wartime experiences, I made a discovery that would change me forever: the ocean. I was elated, transported, uplifted—it was the greatest moment of my life. Up to that time I had never seen the horizon line. My jagged past suddenly seemed to be leveled. The sea, a vast expanse with no factories, no churches, no trenches, and no borders—with enough water to rinse my despair, wash out the past, drown my rancor—was an endless space in which to raft and drift.

I packed my rucksack and walked into life, stepping over prejudices and jumping over a lot of conclusions. These excursions into the real world taught me that we are each of us born with a life sentence (which is easier to survive with a smile), that a conscience is more effective when tortured, and that we rid ourselves of prejudices only to replace them with other ones. I learned to transfuse my fear, insecurity, and anger into my work—trauma can fuel talent, if you have any. The pragmatic vision that I developed, concerning the good and evil in myself and in others, has no definite borderlines. I learned from relativity, which is food for doubt, and doubt is a virtue with enough living space for every imperfect, sin-ridden, life-loving creature on Earth.

The stork is the symbol of Alsace, like me a migrant bird. While this whole building burned down, the twig nest miraculously remained. The storks came back from the North African winter in the spring of 1945 as if nothing had happened. Symbols are sometimes too good to be true. The ecology of the area has since changed, and there are no more frogs for the storks to live on. They are now fed with hamburger meat and winter in Alsace.

TOMI: A CHILDHOOD UNDER THE NAZIS WAS TYPESET IN ADOBE JANSON, A TYPEFACE DEVELOPED AT THE JANSON FOUNDRY IN AMSTERDAM AROUND 1690 AND REVIVED IN 1933 BY THE MERGANTHALER LINOTYPE COMPANY. DESCRIBED BY THE PRINTER HUGH WILLIAMSON AS "OF MEDIUM WIDTH, AND RATHER LARGE ON THE BODY," JANSON GOES WELL WITH EITHER MEAT OR FISH.

Typography and binding design by
ANN W. DOUDEN